This is the first book in English on Italy's leading director, Giorgio Strehler. For the last half century Strehler has been an influential and integral part of European theatrical life as founder of Italy's leading repertory theatre, the Piccolo Teatro in Milan, director of the Paris-based Théâtre de l'Europe and through his opera and theatre productions.

In this detailed study, David Hirst evaluates the particular qualities which typify Strehler's work: the lyrical realism which has become the hallmark of his mature style, the fusion of naturalism, epic theatre, commedia dell'arte and lyric opera, and his gift of interpretation via production. Hirst traces this unique style through Strehler's development from the foundation of the Piccolo to the present day and analyses his productions of Goldoni, Shakespeare, Brecht and Verdi among others.

The book will be of interest to students and teachers of drama, theatre studies, opera history and Italian and German studies as well as to the general reader. It includes a chronology of Strehler's productions and theatre career and contains photographs from key productions.

DIRECTORS IN PERSPECTIVE

General editor: Christopher Innes

Giorgio Strehler

What characterises modern theatre above all is continual stylistic innovation, in which theory and presentation have combined to create a wealth of new forms – naturalism, expressionism, epic theatre and so forth – in a way that has made directors the leading figures rather than dramatists. To a greater extent than is perhaps generally realised, it has been directors who have provided dramatic models for playwrights, though of course there are many different variations in this relationship. In some cases a dramatist's themes challenge a director to create new performance conditions (Stanislavski and Chekhov), or a dramatist turns director to formulate an appropriate style for his work (Brecht); alternatively a director writes plays to correspond with his theory (Artaud), or creates communal scripts out of exploratory work with actors (Chaikin, Grotowski). Some directors are identified with a single theory (Craig), others gave definitive shape to a range of styles (Reinhardt); the work of some has an ideological basis (Stein), while others work more pragmatically (Bergman).

Generally speaking, those directors who have contributed to what is distinctly 'modern' in today's theatre stand in much the same relationship to the dramatic texts they work with as composers do to librettists in opera. However, since theatrical performance is the most ephemeral of the arts and the only easily reproducible element is the text, critical attention has tended to focus on the playwright. This series is designed to redress the balance by providing an overview of selected directors' stage work: those who helped to formulate modern theories of drama. Their key productions have been reconstructed from promptbooks, revues, scene-designs, photographs, diaries, correspondence and – where these productions are contemporary – documented by first-hand description, interviews with the director and so forth. Apart from its intrinsic interest, this record allows a critical perspective, testing ideas against practical problems and achievements. In each case, too, the director's work is set in context by indicating the source of his ideas and their influence, the organisation of his acting company and his relationship to the theatrical or political establishment, so as to bring out wider issues: the way theatre both reflects and influences assumptions about the nature of man and his social role.

Christopher Innes

Giorgio Strehler

DAVID L. HIRST

*Honorary Fellow, University of Birmingham,
Department of Drama*

CAMBRIDGE
UNIVERSITY PRESS

Published by the Press Syndicate of the University of Cambridge
The Pitt Building, Trumpington Street, Cambridge CB2 1RP
40 West 20th Street, New York, NY 10011-4211, USA
10 Stamford Road, Oakleigh, Victoria 3166, Australia

First published 1993

A catalogue record for this book is available from the British Library

Library of Congress cataloguing in publication data

Hirst, David L.
    Giorgio Strehler / David L. Hirst.
        p.   cm. – (Directors in perspective)
    Includes index.
    ISBN 0 521 30768 6.
    1. Strehler, Giorgio, 1921–   – Criticism and interpretation.
I. Title.   II. Series.
PN2688.S8H57   1992
792′.0233′092 – dc20   91-27333 CIP

ISBN 0 521 30768 6 hardback

Transferred to digital printing 2003

Contents

Illustrations

All photographs reproduced by permission of Luigi Ciminaghi.

1   Towards a theatre of humanity

The first ten years at the Piccolo Teatro were ten years of theatrical madness. In ten years we chose, rehearsed and mounted nearly eighty plays. We put them on in our small theatre in Milan, in the open air, in squares, churches, celebrated theatres throughout Italy and all over Europe . . . it was hard work but exhilarating. Our theatre was from the start a poor theatre and it has remained a poor theatre. Initially we had a first-rate group of actors and technicians who decided to stay together. But eventually one of them – or a group – would leave and others would take their place. The history of the Piccolo is that of four or five companies which have constantly alternated, changed, amalgamated; plus those few individuals who have stayed with the theatre for twenty or thirty years. The Piccolo started with a group of friends and has developed into a communal theatre in which the personal relationships are all-important, most of all the strong and enduring friendship between myself and Paolo.

Strehler, 'Schegge di memoria', *Teatro in Europa* 1 (1987), p. 70

Giorgio Strehler's now celebrated production of *The Tempest* opened at the Teatro Lirico in Milan in 1978. At its climax the magician in control of events is profoundly influenced by his servant's unlooked-for sympathy for his victims:

ARIEL: Your charm so strongly works them
          That if you now beheld them your affections
          Would become tender.
PROSPERO: Dost think so, spirit?
ARIEL: Mine would, sir, were I human.

As Ariel (Giulia Lazzarini) hovered tentatively behind her master (Tino Carraro) her phrase: 'se fossi *umana*' had the effect of crystallising the essence of Strehler's theatre. This painful moment of realisation coinciding with an Aristotelian reversal of intentions on the part of the 'wronged duke' formed a powerful dramatic catharsis. As Lazzarini, part Pierrot, part acrobat, part ballerina, glided away – still attached to the clearly visible wire which manipulated all the gyrations of the 'tricksy spirit' – we were forced to consider the implications of Prospero's inhumanity. It was at the same time a Brechtian 'alienation effect' and a theatrical image of great force as the magician and his devoted servant – images of the stage director and his interpreter – shared a moment of revelation on Luciano Damiani's bare sand-covered stage.

'Umano' is the key word in Strehler's approach to theatre. In 1974 he published a collection of essays under the title *Per un teatro umano* which

1

stands alongside Brook's *The Empty Space* or Grotowsky's *Towards a Poor Theatre* as a seminal late-twentieth-century text. Only the lack of an English translation has contributed to the relative obscurity of this Italian director, whose work is little known in Britain. It should be pointed out that the title itself is particularly difficult to translate since the Italian word 'umano' has all the implications of human, humane and humanitarian with their concomitant social and political overtones. It is his concern to explore such values through his productions that has led Strehler again and again to Shakespeare, Goldoni and Brecht. These three dramatists have a fundamental significance to his work. Strehler undertook his first production of *The Tempest* in 1948, the year which had marked his initial confrontation with Shakespeare in *Richard II*. In

1   Giulia Lazzarini as Ariel and Tino Carraro as Prospero in Strehler's production of *The Tempest*, 1978

the previous year, the inaugural season at the Piccolo Teatro in Milan had included his first Goldoni staging: *Arlecchino, the Servant of Two Masters*, a play which he has continued to rework for forty years. He did not undertake a full-scale Brecht production until 1956, when he mounted *The Threepenny Opera*. This staging, which Brecht himself considered superior to his original of 1928, was to lead – shortly after Brecht's death – to Strehler's being offered the directorship of the Berliner Ensemble. Though Brecht is still little performed in Italy, his work has featured constantly in the repertoire of the Piccolo, the version of *Galileo* in 1962 being regarded internationally as something close to perfection. It is significant that Strehler should see a strong link between the human concerns explored by these three playwrights whose subject-matter and styles are so different.

The cosmic dimension of Shakespeare is a far cry from the bourgeois world at the centre of Goldoni's drama, or the analysis of political and social conditions seen through a historical perspective which characterises the mature work of Brecht. Strehler's achievement has been to find powerfully effective theatrical styles appropriate to the performance of these dramatists. He is one of the very few directors outside Germany who has tackled Brecht successfully: his skill resides in his combining a clear awareness of the epic style with a stunning sense of theatre and a profound knowledge of music. His work on Goldoni, one of Italy's few great playwrights, has resulted in a major revaluation of the canon. Not only has Strehler revealed the strengths of previously neglected or underestimated pieces (such as the *Villeggiatura* trilogy or *Le baruffe chiozzotte*) but – along with Dario Fo – he has been responsible for a revival of the commedia style. His interest in Shakespeare – which began, significantly enough, with productions of the major history plays – saw its crowning achievement in his *King Lear* (1972) and his *Tempest*. These two productions employed his vast range of theatrical skills – from commedia through to aspects of epic staging – whilst having an essentially Italian emphasis in their affinity with lyric opera, another field of Strehler's interest and achievement.

Not only has Strehler consistently returned to these three dramatists; he has often returned to the same play. *Arlecchino* has never been out of the Piccolo repertoire for long, having been through six entirely different productions. He has returned to *The Threepenny Opera* twice (in 1973 and 1986) and has reworked Shakespeare's first historical trilogy – as *Il gioco dei potenti* (*Power Games*) – on three separate occasions. Two plays crucial to his theatre – *The Cherry Orchard* and Bertolazzi's *El nost Milan* – both received their first productions in 1955 and were later revived in greatly enriched stagings. In his important study of Strehler's work up to 1965, *Teoria e realtà del Piccolo Teatro di Milano*, Giorgio Guazzotti concludes by suggesting that

Strehler has always been guided by some kind of intuitive 'compass', one which has gradually become more and more precise and which accounts both for the choice of his plays and the style of his work. This is a useful image, complemented by Strehler's own more recent suggestion that very often the plays have forced themselves on him rather as the six characters did on Pirandello. To date Strehler has undertaken some 200 productions. His range is vast and may at first seem bewilderingly eclectic. But it is important to understand from the start the principles which have guided his work and which have gradually emerged with greater clarity over half a century of theatrical activity.

Strehler's name will always be linked to that of the Piccolo, the theatre he helped to found in Milan which celebrated its fortieth anniversary in 1987. Equally important in the story of the Piccolo is Paolo Grassi, Strehler's friend and associate, who helped him found and run the theatre until Strehler broke with the organisation in 1968. The way in which this theatre came into being makes a fascinating story indicative of the cultural and political atmosphere in post-war Italy in general and in Milan in particular. Though Strehler's career has developed considerably since then, the beliefs and principles which led him to undertake that enterprise at the Piccolo still inform the whole of his work.

Strehler was born at Barcola (Trieste) on 14 August 1921, but moved to Milan with his mother in 1928. In 1938 he became a student at the Accademia dei Filodrammatici, where he studied for two years to be an actor. After graduating in June 1940 he worked with a number of theatrical companies – both traditional and experimental – and in January 1943 made his directorial debut with three one-act plays by Pirandello. In September of that year he was called up for military service and spent the last two years of the war in Switzerland, partly in a prisoner-of-war camp at Murren, and then, after receiving permission from the Swiss authorities, in Geneva. He was able to attend classes at the Conservatory there and he went on to found an international company, La Compagnie des Masques, under the pseudonym of Georges Firmy. When the war ended he returned to Milan.

A thriving cultural scene characterised Milan in the period immediately after its liberation by the Allies. The city had been the centre of partisan resistance in the North and the freedom which followed the downfall of the fascist regime influenced the literary life there, creating an intellectual solidarity. As publications such as *Politecnico*, edited by the writer Elio Vittorini, and *Avanti!* gave scope for the exchange of fresh political and social viewpoints, the new theatre was struggling to emerge. Paolo Grassi, then a critic for *Avanti!*, provoked a particularly lively scene in the foyer of the Teatro Nuovo when he accused the play then showing, by Aldo de

Benedetti, of a fascist ideology and referred pointedly to actresses who had been the mistresses of important members of the regime. Outraged defence of Italian womanhood was countered by the young Vittorio Gassman, who leapt on to a chair and – citing Kaiser and Strindberg – announced that the theatre 'must grow up or die'. The celebrated veteran actor Renzo Ricci (Gassman's father-in-law) retorted stiffly: 'You cite Kaiser and Strindberg, but I have performed *Shakespeare*' – which proved too much for Grassi, who burst out: 'You might have performed Shakespeare, but you're an old ham!'[1]

Strehler soon teamed up with Grassi and tried to persuade him to found a theatre company. Grassi, however, believing that something along the lines of a civic public theatre was in the long run more important than any individual enterprise, succeeded in making him bide his time. Strehler in turn became a drama critic – for *Milano Sera* – but was soon drawn back to directing when the veteran experimental director Anton Giulio Bragaglia suggested mounting *Mourning Becomes Electra*. O'Neill's vast drama was performed with great success – after only two weeks of rehearsal – and was followed by stagings of *Desire Under The Elms* and *Thérèse Raquin*. The Zola, with its realistic emphasis, seems in retrospect the most characteristic piece for Strehler to have tackled in this period when he was throwing himself with gusto into whatever theatrical venture offered itself.

His next choice – to mount Gorky's *The Petite Bourgeoisie* – was a more meaningful decision, seconded by Grassi, who set about his first administrative venture with Strehler by finding the necessary funds. It was another Gorky play – *The Lower Depths* – which was to open the memorable first season at the Piccolo the following year; the nucleus of actors was the same in both. Grassi was convinced that the time had come to team up with Strehler in a more ambitious venture and set about looking for a venue. The story of their first visit to the place that was to become their theatre is remarkable. They happened to stop in front of the Cinema Broletto in Via Rovello. During the last months of the war it had been the base for a fascist regiment – the Muti – employed to round up and torture partisans (there was congealed blood on the walls of the ex-dressing rooms, which had served as cells). Immediately after the war it had been taken over as a club for allied soldiers. A notice reading 'Off Limits' was still in evidence when the two men went into the courtyard and saw a door fastened with a small lock. Grassi kicked down the door and they went in. Strehler describes the sight:

An abandoned auditorium with uprooted seats, an empty stage with a red curtain drawn half-way up. Suddenly whilst we were gazing in a thin ray of sunlight crossed the stage and stopped in one corner. It was just as though a spotlight had been switched on almost by magic and a shaft of light was consciously trying to point out the stage: this stage. An invitation? A provocation?[2]

Grassi turned to Strehler and asked: 'Well, Giorgio, do you think you can turn this place into a home for a permanent theatre company?' Strehler stayed in the empty cinema for four hours and thought it through very carefully. He decided to take the risk.

The work during the next few months was intensive: the theatre had to be overhauled and equipped, a programme had to be formulated, a company assembled and the funds for the enterprise found. This was no one-off undertaking by an enthusiastic group of theatricals; Grassi took the matter to the highest level, involving critics, writers and officials. The mayor, Greppi, was enthusiastic and on 29 January 1947 convened a meeting with other cultural and political advisors. There were the usual objections, including that of a noted left-wing figure who claimed that priority should be given to the public services, schools and hospitals; but Montagnani, the cultural representative, argued that 'moral and cultural values are of equal importance to a society as building walls or expanding public services'. This point of view was dear to Grassi, who had claimed in an article in *Avanti!* (25 April 1946) that theatre was itself a 'public service'. Mindful of the achievement of art theatres, notably in Paris and Moscow, Grassi had proposed a different solution for the Milanese situation. He felt it was necessary to start from scratch, to stimulate and provoke the public, to make it conscious of its role and nature: in a word, to *form* it. In his view it was the duty of the public – as well as the state – to use such a public service.

In short Grassi argued that theatre was as necessary, as fundamental, as public transport, the health service or education. His brand of inspired liberal communism struck a chord with Strehler and influenced the formation of the Piccolo – from its choice of repertoire and staff through to the administration. Strehler insists that 'the Piccolo Teatro has always remained faithful to two principles: a free interchange of ideas within the group and a stress on human values in the selection of the repertoire'.[3] The manifesto which was issued to coincide with the first season made Grassi and Strehler's position clear:

After the rhetoric of theatre for the masses and the restrictions of fascist propaganda we believe it is time to begin to work in depth so that later we can gain a wider audience. We hope that the theatre-goers who come to us will become the nucleus who will help to fill bigger theatres; unless we deceive ourselves, every civilisation works by bringing different groups of people together and integrating them into a richer and more varied unit.[4]

They were insistent that the Piccolo should not be an 'experimental' theatre or private institution putting on plays only for the initiated. It would be 'an art theatre for everybody'. They wanted a new audience: workers, young people drawn from schools, the university, offices and factories; and they offered shows 'of a high artistic calibre at prices as low as possible'.

Strehler's task was threefold: to create a new repertoire, a new audience and a new acting style. In this he was assisted by Grassi, who helped to form his social and political commitment, curbed some of the director's wilder excesses, found the money to finance the company's ventures, and proved a

2   Strehler with his co-founder of the Piccolo Teatro, Paolo Grassi

skilful politician in persuading the authorities of the validity of the more ambitious schemes. If the Piccolo has – over forty years – become something of a fashionable institution, this is precisely because Strehler and Grassi have achieved their aim in attracting an ever wider public. The house in Via Rovello was soon to prove far too small to accommodate the ever-expanding audience even after the structural alterations completed in 1952 had expanded the seating for 500 to nearly 700. Various solutions have been sought: from increasing the number of performances to playing in a bigger theatre, the Lirico. But the first expedient inevitably reduces the number of productions per season, whilst the Lirico is acoustically far from ideal as a theatre for straight plays. The only real answer would be a new base. In 1986 the company expanded its work to the Teatro Studio (which also has restricted seating space) and Strehler now increasingly looks to the Odéon in Paris as a base for launching large-scale productions. The Milan authorities – who took twelve years to recognise the theatre's right to the status of 'ente autonomo' (an official state-supported organisation, like La Scala) – have been even slower to construct for the company the theatre it so plainly deserves.

The choice of repertoire for the opening season was crucial. There had been talk of beginning with Machiavelli's *Mandragola*, an Italian classic, but a lawyer, Luigi Meda, acting for the Christian Democrat party, opposed this on the grounds that the play dramatised the violation of one of the sacraments, confession. The inaugural play finally chosen was Gorky's *The Lower Depths*, followed by *The Nights of Rage* by Salacrou, *The Prodigious Magician* by Calderón and Goldoni's *Arlecchino, the Servant of Two Masters*. The repertoire was a deliberate challenge and invitation to the new audience; but it can also be seen at a much later point in time as fulfilling the artistic credo which was guiding the founders and which has continued to influence Strehler for over forty years. If Shakespeare had to wait a little and Brecht a long while, there was Goldoni, represented by the play which was soon to become the company's international hallmark. The Calderón initiated that preoccupation with the magic of theatre which was to grow and mature through Strehler's career. His concern with the life of the lower depths was to recur not only in the revival of the Gorky in 1970 but in his productions of *El nost Milan* and *The Threepenny Opera*. The search for a realistic style appropriate to Italian techniques of acting was already beginning in that first show. The Salacrou (another piece he was to revive, in 1964) is a play about the French Resistance, of particular significance to a Milanese audience in the immediate post-war period. Special performances were given for ex-partisans; it must have been a disturbing experience for them to visit – or revisit – the place which had once been the base of their arch-enemies, the Muti.

The choice of repertoire was only one aspect of the challenge – it implied a certain type of audience, but that audience had to be educated, encouraged to expand their theatrical tastes. More to the point, Strehler had to find a group of actors – new actors – and train them in an acting style (or styles) which he would have to invent. As he has pointed out:

We were a generation without teachers, without leaders. We were kids who had nurtured a love for theatre, but at a great distance because we had grown old somewhere else, in a war that was for so many of us a source of great unhappiness or for others the excuse for mad, empty rhetoric. We were young in years, though, and in human and theatrical experience. And we were the ones who were going to have to guide 'the others'. These 'others' lived apart in a world of their own in which their way of working, their whole approach to theatre had grown decadent. They were profoundly cut off from reality in every sense; they knew neither the words to speak nor the way to speak them. They were trying to keep alive a theatre which both from a historical and a human point of view was at least fifty years out of date.[5]

What Strehler says his generation lacked were 'maestri': men of practical experience and knowledge who could teach and inspire them. In fact in a later essay entitled 'I miei maestri' (in *Per un teatro umano*) he points to three men who had a formative influence on him: Brecht, Copeau and Jouvet.

Tragically Brecht died shortly after visiting Milan to attend rehearsals and the performance of *The Threepenny Opera*, so that the friendship and admiration which had grown between the two men was not destined to develop. Strehler has expressed regret that he waited so long before he tackled a Brecht play, but his decision was a careful and wise one. Brecht has had the most direct and permanent influence of any writer or director on Strehler; their brief collaboration confirmed Strehler's interest and skills, which have expanded ever since. Strehler paid eloquent tribute to Jouvet when he mounted *Elvire or A Passion for Theatre*, in 1986, his dramatic adaptation of the French director's lectures on theatre given at the Conservatoire in Paris just before he left France for South America in 1940. Strehler has said:

As a young enthusiastic boy of twenty I learnt from him that theatre is a day-to-day joy, not a divine art. I owe to Jouvet in particular the sense of a critical imagination working within a show. The discovery that a production isn't just a philological, technical or cultural undertaking, but also a living interpretation of the text, an intuitive acceptance of its poetic values.[6]

He invited Jouvet to Italy when he fell out of favour in France after the failure of his *Tartuffe* production; Jouvet responded by helping the Piccolo when they went to France later – in 1949 – inviting the whole of fashionable Paris to their shows and introducing a radio programme in which Strehler talked about commedia. Strehler's debt to Copeau (whom he never met) is explained as follows:

I owe to Copeau an austere, moral, almost Jansenist vision of theatre. Theatre representing moral responsibility in a collective context. A painfully religious feeling for theatre. I believe that deep down Copeau abandoned the theatre because he'd come to realise that in order to perform theatre as he wanted it performed he would have had to demand of his cast and crew the sort of things only God can require.[7]

His admiration for Copeau stems from the fact that the ex-director of the Vieux Colombier retired to Burgundy: 'to carry on his battle against star actors and to find a performance style that would be at the service of the text.'[8]

Despite his rejection of the ethics and aesthetics of the outmoded style of performance which reached its nadir during the fascist regime, Strehler has always had a great admiration for the talented veteran actors of a previous generation. Many of them have responded by working at the Piccolo: Camillo Pilotto (Strehler's first Prospero and Falstaff), Renzo Ricci (Richard III), Sarah Ferrati (Bernarda Alba) and Wanda Capodaglio (Volumnia), for example. Strehler was shrewd enough to learn from these 'maestri' too, whilst they, in working with him, developed their skills. As he has pointed out:

How many great actors and actresses who had become famous in the 1930s came to act with us, to put themselves in step with the new movements (even if that isn't quite what they would have admitted)? It would be unfair and historically inaccurate to claim that we in Via Rovello have ever run a theatre *opposed* to actors. We did – it's true – get rid of the excesses of the star actor.[9]

One of the main reasons for his sense of pride, Strehler claims, is that the Piccolo has always been there as 'a house you set off from and to which you came back ... a springboard ... or a port where you could refuel after a long voyage'. An anecdote which illustrates Strehler's down-to-earth practicality as a director – which he had already learned in part from Jouvet and which he was to develop through his encounter with Brecht – explains one of the fundamental reasons for his early (and continued) success with actors. Lilla Brignone, who had been with the company from the first season and who had played many roles including the Nurse in *Romeo and Juliet*, Viola, Nora in *A Doll's House* and Katherina in *The Taming of the Shrew*, was cast as Electra in Sophocles' tragedy (Strehler's only production of a classical Greek play to date). She felt out of her depth, frightened of making a fool of herself, and in a moment of exasperation banged on Strehler's directing table and shouted: 'Why the hell are we performing this rubbish anyway?' Instead of playing the indignant young intellectual, Strehler used all his skill and knowledge of the profession to cajole her into continuing with the difficult role. 'I had acted myself', he says, 'played walk-on parts, taken the prima donna's dog for a pee, toured in the provinces. I knew all about the poverty and the nobility of the profession. I was in a position to understand the problem.'[10] Strehler's histrionic skills are impressive – as anyone who has seen him in rehearsal will acknowledge. He could have had a highly successful career as an actor.

The aim – expressed in the manifesto of 1947 – of working in depth so as to win a wider audience was more completely realised when the swift turnover of Strehler's productions slowed down and he was able to work on the plays in more detail. The overwhelming success of his *Galileo* in 1963 was in large part due to seventy days of rehearsal, the period he had by then come to see as necessary for a work of such dialectical complexity. This was a very different procedure from that which characterised the first few years at the Piccolo. Those early programmes were necessarily eclectic in that the company was exploring a wide variety of authors and styles, albeit governed by the belief that 'theatre above all should look for its *raison d'être* in society, tackling real down-to-earth problems, always acting as an instrument which is capable of interpreting society'.[11] Although ever since that first season the Piccolo has employed other directors, Strehler was from the start the central focus of the work; he gave the programme its direction: ideas were worked out through practice and experiment and distinguished by his need to discover poetry in the theatrical medium, his keen social sense and the consciousness that the company was helping to mould and influence a new Italian society.

The pace of work in those formative years was hectic and the number and variety of the plays mounted impressive. By the 1950–1 and 1951–2 seasons Strehler was regularly undertaking between ten and a dozen productions a year at the Piccolo as well as five at La Scala. His range was extraordinary: Shakespeare, Goldoni, Sophocles, Ibsen, Molière, Eliot, Büchner on the one hand; Strauss, Donizetti, Malipiero and Massenet on the other. Significantly enough, a decade later, in the 1962–3 season, during which *Galileo* was mounted, the only other productions he undertook were a further Brecht – *Mahagonny* – at La Scala and new versions of two of the plays from the inaugural season: *The Nights of Rage* and *Arlecchino*. The pattern was beginning to emerge much more clearly: the Piccolo style and repertoire was beginning to crystallise. *Galileo* was Strehler's first show that season; he had worked on it from the previous autumn until it opened in April and then ran for two months. It effectively took up the whole season. It was revived the following November and ran for another four months in Milan before playing in Rome for a further two. With this production the in-depth work could be seen to bear fruit in a staging which was seen by a much wider section of the public.

Ugo Ronfani tells us: 'The theatre for Strehler is the opposite of a place of rest. Rather in its ephemeral quality, in its ever-changing and contradictory nature as *dream, mirage, magic* lies its fascination and nobility. Even when it aspires to the universal, the theatre – according to Strehler – must pass through the *here* and *now*, the *hic et nunc*.'[12] Ronfani has in mind the 'trilogy of illusion' (*The Tempest*, Corneille's *L'Illusion* and Eduardo de Filippo's *La grand magia*) but the obsessive theme which Strehler has recently translated into three stunning theatrical variations has always been a pressing concern. As a man of the theatre Strehler is necessarily haunted by the realisation that theatre's particular strength, to express complex truths with visual and verbal clarity, is fleeting and transitory. It is in an attempt to combat the reality of this fact that Strehler has so assiduously revived shows, reworked them, revised them, and been responsible for the company's lengthy and some-times gruelling tours in Italy and abroad. The first of these took Gozzi's *The Crow* to London and Paris in 1949; by 1956 *Arlecchino* and *Tonight We Improvise* were taken on a three-month tour comprising forty-one perfor-mances at nineteen cities in Britain, Sweden, Finland, Denmark, Norway, Austria and East Germany. Through these strategies Strehler has tried to give his theatrical creations an extended lifespan and influence.

In the volume published ten years after the formation of the Piccolo Strehler could say: 'the history of our shows can be written in relation to our constant search for themes and trends which at this point in time more clearly manifest themselves as developments and achievements'.[13] This was in 1958. The *Villeggiatura* trilogy and the third edition of *Arlecchino* had already established Strehler's genius as a director of Goldoni; his *Coriolanus* (1957) had set the seal on his reputation as a Shakespeare interpreter, and – coming as it did between *The Threepenny Opera* and *The Good Person of Setzuan* – it served to point up the link between Shakespeare and Brecht, whose style Strehler had mastered in those first two shows. The consequence of pursuing an ethical and aesthetic programme which is mounted on the three pillars of Brecht, Goldoni and Shakespeare – all writers passionately concerned with social issues whose stress on human values implies a faith in mankind – is that certain key European dramatists will be inevitably marginalised. It was no secret that Grassi was strongly opposed to the Absurdist theatre of Beckett and Ionesco; significantly, it was not until after his death that Strehler mounted *Happy Days* – in 1982. When Ronfani in his interview tries to draw Strehler on the significance of this long wait, the director sidesteps, cunningly citing a comment of Brecht remembered from the last conver-sation he had with him in Berlin: '"Do you know"– he told me – "I'd like to stage *Waiting for Godot*. I'm not quite sure how yet, but I'm thinking about it. There's just one thing" – he added mischievously – "where were Vladimir and Estragon during the Second World War?"'[14] It is not that Strehler is lacking in reasons for mounting a Beckett play – or indeed Genet's *The*

Balcony, which he directed in 1976 with a marked emphasis on its analysis of power – but that his critics and audience have been less easily won over by these works.

His interest in Pirandello is more complex and problematic. In 1965 Giorgio Guazzotti could confidently dismiss Strehler's Pirandello productions as anomalies, relegating them to a position of insignificance along with his stagings of modern French existentialist dramas, which in their nihilistic philosophy express what he terms a 'mimed lack of commitment' ('mimetizzato qualunquismo'). Odoardo Bertani, writing an important article on Strehler's Pirandello productions in 1987, could not take Guazzotti's stand, largely because of the major significance of Strehler's staging of *The Mountain Giants* in 1966, the year after Guazzotti's study was published.

Though there have been long periods when Pirandello has been out of the Piccolo repertoire (nothing since the 1966 *Mountain Giants* until *As You Desire Me* in 1988), it cannot be said that Strehler has neglected his work. His first theatrical undertaking was a triple bill of his one-act plays, and he has directed two of the plays in the trilogy concerned with the ambiguous relationship between theatre and life (*Tonight We Improvise* and *Six Characters In Search of An Author*) – a basic theme of Strehler's own work. *The Mountain Giants* – Pirandello's last and uncompleted work – has affinities with *The Tempest* in its story of the magician and the group of actors who perform for him. This production of the work was Strehler's third (the first being at the Piccolo in 1947, the second in Düsseldorf in 1958) and it ranks among the finest of all his stagings. Not having approached Pirandello in the preceding eight years, his return to *The Mountain Giants* in 1966 seemed charged with significance: most particularly at the conclusion of the play. The actors, having mimed Pirandello's scenario for the uncompleted last act, exit leaving their cart on the stage. At this point the heavy metallic safety-curtain crashed down, smashing the cart. Strehler did not direct another play at the Piccolo for six years, leaving his old theatre in 1968 and returning in 1972. His final gesture in *The Mountain Giants* was to prove a chilling anticipation of what lay ahead.

'The iron safety curtain which smashed the actors' cart didn't symbolise for me the end of theatre', Strehler remarked later, 'it represented the death of a dream, one I had pursued and defended for twenty years in the face of increasing opposition. I had to start again from scratch.'[15] Strehler was experiencing a period of intense disillusionment in the late sixties. He felt he was further than ever from realising his idea of a public theatre; financial subsidy was proving insufficient and there was no sign of a new venue. He has explained that vital sections of local government and state administration had become so over-politicised as to be ineffective; the authorities were little interested in culture in general and theatre in particular; theatre did not function as a public service. His sense of frustration and betrayal was shared by the students and workers who in 1968 combined forces to challenge the *status quo* and the government. The 'contestazione' – as it became known – was the Italian manifestation of a phenomenon which had broken out on American university campuses a few years previously and was now beginning to affect all parts of Europe. After its post-war recovery Italy had lived through the economic boom of the late fifties and early sixties, and was now experiencing a recession: the 'dolce vita' was coming to an end. This angry but determined spirit of political enquiry was affecting the theatre: in 1968 Dario Fo and Franca Rame left the commercial theatre circuit, formed a more egalitarian co-operative and worked through Communist party venues in direct contact with workers and students.

'The *contestazione* taught me a terrible lesson', Strehler admits: 'to discover one morning that you're right-wing, in the eyes of many a reactionary, when only the night before you thought you were well to the left, fighting for the cause.'[16] He admits that such a disturbing awakening, which triggered in him the need to reassess his political position in relation to his work and which was to result in his quitting the Piccolo, had its origins in a growing disillusionment and a need for change. The revelation was triggered off, however, by a particular incident during that turbulent year, 1968. One morning, hearing voices outside the window, he looked out and saw a band of students shouting slogans and carrying banners and red flags. 'They're at it early, I thought; I wonder who they've got it in for?' he asked. He soon found out: 'They had it in for *me*; the banners and shouts left no room for doubt: "Down with the tyrant of the Piccolo!" "Down with the baron of the stage!" "Get rid of the monster!" "Get off your throne!"' Strehler suggested they all go along to the theatre; he got dressed (elegantly – he points out – 'not in a red shirt and badly-creased trousers like some pseudo-revolutionary') and held a public meeting at the Piccolo with the demonstrators alongside theatre staff and technicians. Then he took one of the marchers into his office, pointed to his armchair – the infamous 'throne' – told him he could have it, and left.

The gesture was in Strehler's best theatrical vein, but it was sincere. Countering the gibe of the film critic Tullio Kezich, who accused him of quitting his job in a fit of pique over the complaints of a few students, he points out that he felt the need to work in a different environment; 'to carry on a certain type of debate which didn't seem to me to be possible any longer within certain institutions which had become too rigid and atrophied'.[17] He formed the *Gruppo Teatro e Azione*, designed to explore more urgent political issues in a different theatrical context. The contrast with Dario Fo is telling. Though the group's manifesto talks of performing in factories to an audience 'perhaps ideologically closer to us', they never did this. They played in well-known theatres – the Quirino in Rome, the Teatro della Pergola in Florence and the Lirico in Milan. There was no real attempt to create a co-operative with everyone on an equal footing in terms of wages and casting (a mistake Fo and Rame made, and were soon to correct); the company comprised essentially people who had worked at the Piccolo; the shows were designed by Frigerio with music by Carpi.

There were four shows, all with a marked political content: *The Song of the Lusitanian Bogey* (1969) by Peter Weiss, *St Joan of the Stockyards* (1970), *The Lower Depths* (1970) and *Referendum as to the Pardon or Reprieve of a War Criminal* (1971) by Roberto Pallavicini and Gian Franco Vene. The first and fourth were the most hard-hitting, Weiss's dramatisation of third-world issues causing several outbursts from the audience at the premiere in Rome. We are dealing here with a phase of Strehler's work parallel to that of Peter Brook in the same period. *US* was shocking audiences at the Aldwych not expecting this type of work from the Royal Shakespeare Company. When asked why he felt the need to direct the Weiss, Strehler argued that it was necessary to force people to see the truth: 'the truth should always be shouted out loud. Everywhere', but he adds, characteristically: 'One thing, though, make sure you shout it out with style!' Even in this, his most overtly committed period of direction, Strehler did not overlook either the poetic or theatrical force of the work. This was the case most notably in his staging of *St Joan of the Stockyards*, another landmark in his dialogue with Brecht.

Of the *Gruppo Teatro e Azione* enterprise he has commented: 'the most important thing is to have firm principles, get on with changing social and theatrical institutions, not so much in a spirit of simplistic reforming zeal, but rather as a daily tactical struggle which is part of a bigger strategic battle'.[18] His return to the Piccolo in 1972 was in no sense a retrograde step; rather, he had taken stock of the situation and was, moreover, in a position to make demands which were designed to effect just such reforms as were necessary to bring his idea of a true public theatre nearer reality. He was offered the sole directorship of the Piccolo, which he accepted on certain very clear terms: that the Milanese authorities guarantee a more whole-hearted commitment, that the company's debts be written off, that a new home be found as soon as possible, and that he be allowed to organise a programme that was 'intensive' rather than 'extensive' – that the commercial pressures be taken off so that he could explore the repertoire in greater depth.

Not all these conditions were faithfully respected, but a more supportive attitude by the authorities has facilitated the policy which has governed his work in the last two decades. One trend is dominant in this period: a constant return to those plays which for him are most meaningful so as to reinterpret them for another generation of actors and theatre-goers. The proof of his maturity is most evident in these revivals, which in Strehler's case are not so much restagings as further reflections on the works which at each undertaking deepen in meaning and effectiveness. *The Threepenny Opera, Il gioco dei potenti, The Cherry Orchard*, the *Villeggiatura* trilogy, *The Good Person of Setzuan* and — most importantly — *Arlecchino* have all gone through a sea-change during the years since his return to the Piccolo. Another pointer to his method is the recent 'trilogy of illusion' comprising *The Tempest*, Corneille's *L'Illusion* and Eduardo de Filippo's *La grande magia*. All three were landmarks in Strehlerian staging, receiving universal critical praise and setting the seal on the integration of his mature style whilst at the same time pointing back to significant phases in his career.

It is worth considering what these three productions had in common: they tell us a great deal about Strehler's theatre in the late eighties. None of these plays is straightforward, either for the audience or the director. *The Tempest* is an acknowledged masterpiece, but the complexity and richness of the play are very difficult to realise in performance. Both the Corneille and the de Filippo dramas have enjoyed little or no success in the theatre: Corneille famously referred to the play as an 'étrange monstre' (it was written just before *Le Cid* and is a much more volatile amalgam of theatrical genres); Louis Jouvet — whose 1937 production at the Comédie-Française remains a crucial reference-point for Strehler — told him that he thought *L'Illusion* was in some mysterious way bewitched. Eduardo de Filippo's *La grande magia* (*Great Magic*), written in 1948, is the Neapolitan writer's blackest and least characteristic play, one which soon dropped out of the repertoire. It is a measure of Strehler's achievement not only to have triumphed with a difficult play in the Shakespeare canon, but to have displayed the strengths of two other dramas hitherto relegated to positions of inferiority. He has inspired a major revaluation of the European repertoire: indeed the term 'repertoire' becomes more significant when we recognise that Strehler has vindicated in practice the theatrical force and effectiveness of plays which dramatic criticism has tended to underestimate or misunderstand.

This is an unusual virtue in a director, and is perhaps the most significant clue to Strehler's theatrical genius. He has often expressed regret that his commitment to theatre denied him the opportunity to work as an orchestral conductor, for which his musical training and skills qualify him. For instance, when working with him on *Pelléas and Mélisande* at La Scala in 1949, Victor de Sabata, the celebrated musical director, urged Strehler: 'You were made to conduct an orchestra; leave the Piccolo, come and work with me, and after three years you'll be a conductor'.[19] He would also have made a great critic — he worked as a journalist in the mid-forties until he abandoned this for directing. Indeed he *is* a great critic, as his own writings testify; moreover it is his skill in combining critical insight and theatrical inspiration which is at the heart of his talent: 'I have always known', he commented to Ugo Ronfani, 'that I was a born interpreter. Not a creator. But not an interpreter who works on his own. Someone who works within a group'.[20]

We are dealing here, then, with a phenomenon very different from Peter Brook (to whom the playwright's text is of minimal importance now) or Peter Stein (whose concern with theatrical style is a creative end in itself). Still less are we dealing with a director like Luca Ronconi – the only figure of comparable stature in Italy – an artist whose choice of theatrical works is determined more by their potential for realising his own imaginative skills than by any need to interpret them. Though Strehler is a director of phenomenal theatrical talent, his choice of plays has always been determined by a necessity to interpret the piece and by an intuitive and imaginative feeling for the links and relationships between works. He is first and foremost an interpreter; however striking his theatrical productions (particularly in recent years) may have been, they have always proved a source of illumination – and often revaluation – of the dramatic text.

Thus the three plays forming the trilogy – *The Tempest*, *L'Illusion* and *La grande magia* – though quite different in content, representing three different countries at contrasted points in time – were united in representing certain aspects of Strehler's theatrical style characteristic of this phase in his career. All three captured that elusive quality of tragi-comic lyricism which is a particular hallmark of his recent theatre. All three had settings of exquisite beauty and stunning theatrical effectiveness. Strehler's ultra-sensitive aware-ness of language, both in terms of the written text and its vocal delivery, was marked. A subtle and brilliantly articulated humour informed all three shows. The acting was distinguished by performances of total psychological conviction, though they might be expressed through a variety of perfor-mance styles ranging from commedia through to neo-classical heroic acting. In all three productions he inspired performances of extraordinary individual force and versatility, either from veteran actors such as Tino Carraro and Renato de Carmine (Otto Maravuglia in *La grande magia*) or from newcomers such as the young television star Eleonora Brigliadori (in the de Filippo play) or Gérard Desarthe pulling off a *coup de théâtre* by doubling the magician Alcandre and the braggart captain Matamore in *L'Illusion*. Actors love Strehler. His achievement has always been to extend their skills within the context of a carefully-thought-out and wholly original production.

I was fortunate enough to see all of these shows; and on several occasions. They have left me with a very clear impression of Strehler's style and theatri-cal interests. His 1978 production of *The Tempest* begs some interesting questions as to what constitute the strengths of the play. Since he was working from a translation (a brilliant one by Agostino Lombardo), the verbal felicities of the original gave way to an emphasis on the Italianate features of the drama: its setting, the element of pastoral romance peculiar to the tragi-comic world of Guarini, the comic scenes (undoubtedly derived from commedia routines) and the Pirandellian sense of theatre-within-theatre, an interplay of reality and illusion. The whole production, from its stunning opening scene of shipwreck through to the collapse of the set followed by its miraculous reformation at the end of Prospero's epilogue, explored the ethical concepts of the play – in particular the analysis of the nature and effect of power – through a sequence of startlingly powerful theatrical images.

The production of L'Illusion matched this. It opened with Pridamant and his friend Dorant walking through the audience and onto the stage where they encountered the magician Alcandre in his cave. As Pridamant confessed to Alcandre his guilt at having exiled his son, the magician transformed the cave – in Strehler's production – into a Platonic grotto in which the anguished father was able to observe the adventures of his son. The theatrical illusion is two-fold: it is expressed through the magician's skill and through the effect in the final act when the father, thinking he has observed his son's death, is made to see that it was all a theatrical trick – Clindor has joined a group of actors. The scenery disappears and we are shown the company sharing the evening's proceeds before going off. Strehler's innovation – making Pridamant unable to cross from the auditorium on to the stage to embrace his son – was the final twist on the play's central concern with reality and illusion. This was further explored in the casting. Strehler employed a group of seven actors to play twelve parts; the doubling was significant, notably that of Nada Strancar as the maid, Lyse, and the English princess, Rosine, and of Gérard Desarthe as the magician and the captain. By this device Strehler created a series of mirror reflections within the play, deepening its ambiguities.

Though the Pirandellian theatrical features were significant – several critics compared the production to Strehler's celebrated production of *The Mountain Giants* in 1966 – his decision to employ Corneille's revised title of 1660 (the original version of 1636 was called *L'Illusion comique*, i.e. *The Theatrical Illusion*) emphasised his belief in the fact that the subject of the drama is the complex tangle of psychological and emotional issues which constitute the illusion basic to Corneille's study. As Strehler put it: 'what struck me was this metaphor of life where theatre is employed as a poetic and disturbing demonstration of the relativity of the relationships of the characters who play out this human adventure on a world stage'.[21] Emilia

3   Gérard Desarthe as Matamore and Marc Delsaert as Clindor in Corneille's
     L'Illusion, 1984

Lodigiani observed in *Libertà* (24 November 1984) that the braggart captain Matamore became the most significant figure: 'an example of the character who always treats life as a stage – and alongside him, his counterpart, the wizard, Alcandre: an image of the author whose real magic consists in understanding the secrets of the human heart and in revealing them through his narrative'. In this production Alcandre's cave was not a place of empty shadows: white magic – akin to that of Prospero – made it an instrument for discovery and learning. What Alcandre showed to the distressed father, Pridamant, and thereby to the audience, was a fantastic panorama of scenes realised with rare theatrical refinement in Ezio Frigerio's Fragonard- and Watteau-inspired settings:

autumnal woods and palaces in the background are illuminated by an ambiguous deceptive daylight, whilst chiaroscuro effects break up the dominant nocturnal gloom of the front stage. The rocky opening of the cave frames the action throughout. An evocative transparent screen and a shiny black marble floor create reflections, which flicker just for a moment: the fleeting allusion is to Plato's cave.[22]

As a companion-piece to *The Tempest* this made fascinating and thought-provoking theatre. Though, as Renato Palazzi observed in the *Corriere della sera* (13 April 1984), Strehler's Alcandre was no Prospero or Cotrone (the magician of Pirandello's *The Mountain Giants*), being rather a performer ready to don the false nose of the comic captain, 'an actor who uses theatre to portray the fragility of human passions', both plays gained by comparison with each other in their focus on the contrasting central figures.

When Strehler went on a year later to mount *La grande magia* he extended his examination of theatrical illusion and its relationship to life through his dramatisation of the conjurer, Otto Maravuglia. His choice of this neglected Eduardo de Filippo comedy was a particularly apt tribute to the Neapolitan dramatist, who died just as the play went into rehearsal. It tells the story of Calogero di Spelto, whose young and beautiful wife deserts him, disappearing in earnest at the climax of a presumed conjuring trick and leaving the embarrassed magician to invent the implausible story that she remains closed in a magic box which Calogero may open only when he firmly believes in her fidelity. The piece is entirely characteristic of de Filippo's idiosyncratic genius though in no way typical of his more popular work. It is no surprise to learn that though he revised it more than once, it met with little success, or that it should appeal strongly to Strehler on account of its subject-matter and its challenge to his directorial skills.

Though having strong thematic links with the two previous plays of the trilogy, Strehler's *La grande magia* was in style and theatrical effect wholly original. Eric Bentley in his shrewd and sympathetic analysis of the play is at pains to dispel the idea which in part contributed to its lack of critical success: that it was too heavily influenced by Pirandello. Strehler's production vindicated the individual strengths of the work whilst at the same time ingeniously solving another problem implicit in de Filippo's theatre: its Neapolitan origin and setting. As Enrico Fiore has rightly argued: 'Eduardo was finally recognised universally once he had become a national figure and because before that he was Neapolitan; in short he was great precisely because he was deeply rooted in his Neapolitan origins.' (*Il mattino*, 7 April 1985). Strehler would agree, but the staging – his only one to date of a de Filippo work – whilst stressing the importance of dialect, removed the play from its Neapolitan setting, presenting it instead in a windswept Adriatic spa (along the lines of Fellini's Rimini), and employed the highly original technique of exploiting a variety of dialect accents in the cast: thus the magician was from Rome, his assistant Milanese, the lover Sicilian; only the servant, Gennarino, retained his Neapolitan origins. The effect was to universalise the play. It delighted the Italian (Milanese) audience, who responded to its evocation of a period and a mood (we are again in the realm of tragi-comedy, here given a sentimental twist) and who recognised the genuine worth of a neglected classic. The conjurer's magical effects were brought off with the brio of the director who had delighted audiences with the staging devices of *The Tempest* and *L'Illusion*. Strehler's versatility was once more in evidence, as he was dealing here with the seedy ambience of a charlatan and his tricking of his bourgeois clients. Again, however, the central theme of illusion and power was pursued with a down-to-earth force evident in the directness of the acting, which exposed the sordid – and ultimately pessimistic – aspects of the tale.

The Tempest was the production Strehler chose to open the first season of the Théâtre de l'Europe in Paris in 1983, though his first new production with the company there proved to be *L'Illusion* in the following year. The international dimension of Strehler's work deserves mention at this point. It was a big step for him to move to Paris almost forty years after the formation of the Piccolo and take over the direction of a project designed to develop theatrical collaboration in Europe by breaking down cultural boundaries. Initially Spain (Madrid), France (Paris) and Italy (Milan) were involved in an exchange programme designed to give greater scope and flexibility to directors and actors whilst researching an international language for theatre. Strehler did not abandon Milan; he extended the scope of his activities. Though he had mounted productions in foreign languages abroad, they had most significantly been reworkings of previous triumphs: the *Villeggiatura* trilogy at the Vienna Burgtheater (1974) and at the Comédie-Française (1978); and his *Gioco dei potenti* in Salzburg (1973). His career as an opera director had also taken him outside Italy on several occasions. But the production of *L'Illusion* – in French with a predominantly young company – was a more daring step. Critics (French as well as Italian) marvelled at his liberation of the formal Alexandrines from the stiff conventions established through years of tradition and applauded the expressive physical performances of his actors. Here was a fresh approach which, whilst remaining absolutely faithful to the dramatic features of the play, gave an Italian emphasis to a French classic. Just as he had universalised *La grande magia* by eliminating its Neapolitan features through that sleight of hand which the critic Renzo Tian described as the equivalent of pulling the tablecloth away and leaving the crockery intact, so he had again brought a difficult and neglected work to a wider international public.

Guazzotti – in 1965 – claimed: 'The Piccolo Teatro of Milan was recognised as "European" before it was accepted as a "national" one.' From its earliest years the Piccolo had toured abroad, and it was celebrated for the breadth of its repertoire. But it would be fair to claim that Strehler's theatre is first Milanese and only secondly Italian. Italy does not have a national theatre, a factor which is relevant to Strehler's career in Milan and abroad. Italy has produced few playwrights of international stature, and we need only consider Goldoni, Pirandello, Eduardo de Filippo and Dario Fo to observe that, significantly enough, all four writers come from different parts of the country: Venice, Sicily, Naples and Lombardy respectively. Their geographical and cultural roots are vitally important in their work. If Italy is still a divided country – the administration is in Rome, the commercial centre is Milan, industry centres on the triangle of Milan, Genoa and Turin – the positive side is the pride in local and regional cultures as well as the fierce determination (a post-war, anti-fascist inheritance) to preserve and develop individual dialects.

Strehler's work cannot be understood out of this context any more than his originality and achievement can be fully appreciated without knowing something about the theatrical conditions operating in Italy. The native theatrical culture of Italy is that of lyric opera: this affects all aspects of stage performance from acting style through audience response to assumptions as to what constitutes the dramatic experience. Strehler is not alone in working with ease in both the straight theatre and the opera house (young directors in Britain are currently showing a welcome versatility in this respect); Visconti had this skill, as do Ronconi and Zeffirelli today. The *diva* is still a familiar figure in Italian theatre, as is the *mattatore* or actor-manager. Despite the work of Strehler and the new movements he was in large part responsible for inspiring in the late forties, little has changed in the main body of the Italian theatre. The tendency is still to tour; a production is mounted and then plays the main cities. The company still revolves around the star performer, much as it did in the days of Eleonora Duse: either a glamorous figure like Vittorio Gassman or Gabriele Lavia or a comedian like Dario Fo. Early in his career Strehler established a very different type of theatre, which he has gone on to develop and expand. His achievement is twofold: it resides in his initial pioneering determination to revolutionise theatrical taste as well as in his ability both to refine and to extend the scope of his own theatrical practice.

It is revealing in this context to compare Strehler's career with that of Peter Brook, his close contemporary. Having established himself as the 'enfant terrible' of British theatre in the 1940s, Brook went on to consolidate his reputation in the 1950s, notably with his productions of *Titus Andronicus* (with the Oliviers) and *The Tempest* (with Gielgud). The 1960s proved for him – as for Strehler – a period of crisis and reorientation. His exploration of Artaudian theatrical techniques via his 'theatre of cruelty' workshops gave rise to his production of Weiss's *Marat/Sade* whilst influencing the more controversial shows, *US* and *Oedipus* (the Seneca version) for the RSC and the National Theatre respectively. His collaboration with the poet Ted Hughes led him to search for a new theatrical language of sound and gesture independent of the written text. This took him to the Middle East (for *Orghast*) and Africa (for *The Ik*). His research – now based in Paris – has produced a very different approach to text from that of Strehler. Though he has more recently directed and adapted classics from *Timon of Athens* and *Antony and Cleopatra* through to Bizet's *Carmen*, he continues to search for radically new techniques of vocal and physical expression. His recent staging of the epic *Mahabharata*, which has been mounted in a variety of open-air venues, is his latest attempt to revitalise theatrical ritual.

Strehler's aims are different and his emphasis, by contrast, is well illustrated by his production of Pirandello's *As You Desire Me* (1988). Strehler's own concern to give an international dimension to theatrical language employed a novel device in this staging, first seen in Milan but mounted for the Théâtre de l'Europe. In the first act, set in Berlin, he cast German actors in the roles of Salter and his daughter, Mop. This had the effect of adding to the psychological and spiritual disorientation of the central character, L'Ignota (the Unknown Woman), who is unsure which of the two lives forced on her – in Germany and Italy – she should choose. It became more than a struggle between the truth of the past and that of the present in the production; the theme of illusion versus reality was given an added political dimension in a version of the play which sought to explore the predicament of a woman who discovers that she has no firm roots in either a psychological or cultural sense. The play brought Strehler's German wife, Andrea Jonasson, back to the Piccolo in a role which allowed her to exploit her skill in two languages as well as confirming her previous triumph there in another role of dual identity: the heroine of *The Good Person of Setzuan*.

Strehler's most recent undertaking, a production of Goethe's *Faust*, has proved his most ambitious to date. Taking a selection of scenes from Part I, he mounted his first two experimental evenings of 'fragments' in the 1988–89 season. The project was completed in 1992 when selections from both parts of the play were put together in four two-hour shows. The final result, whilst illustrating the poetic and philosophical strengths of the text, and giving rise to a series of powerful theatrical effects, revealed that the two-part epic – with the exception of the prison scene at the conclusion of Part I (stunningly performed by Giulia Lazzarini) – is lacking in dramatic interest. Strehler himself played Faust. His citing of the hero's words to the company when he first launched the project stand as an explicit credo which has informed his work from the very beginning of his career:

> I feel the courage to take on the world
> to endure the torments of the earth
> and all the earth's great joys;
> to face up to tempests
> and in the midst of shipwreck not to tremble.

4   Andrea Jonasson as The Unknown Woman in Pirandello's *As You Desire Me*, 1988

2   Strehler's style: lyrical realism

Ronfani: The very fact that you tell me you are still looking for a synthesis of Brecht and Stanislavski, and feel committed to this line of research makes me think you don't lay claim to an individual 'method'.
Strehler: If a 'Strehler method' does exist I'm not the one to talk about it. I have never managed to define a personal approach that sets my work apart from that of other directors. or rather, I've never felt the need to do so. Such a method undoubtedly exists, however: it is there in the day-to-day practice of my work.

From Ugo Ronfani, *Io, Strehler: Conversazioni con Ugo Ronfani*, p. 192

The distinguishing feature of Strehler's mature style is a meticulously researched lyrical realism. If during his first years at the Piccolo his choice of texts was eclectic, responding to the need to establish the tastes of a new public – a choice which in turn implied experiment in acting techniques – by the time the basic lines of the repertoire had been laid down a corresponding clarity of performance style had emerged. Strehler's approach was that of fusion: an amalgamation of techniques which remains to this day his hallmark as a director. His later productions of Brecht, Shakespeare and Goldoni are rich in levels of significance, highly complex exercises in theatrical style. Of particular importance is Strehler's naturalistic – or realistic – emphasis, one which in combining Stanislavskian techniques with those familiar from epic theatre extends the resonances of the plays into a poetic evocation of striking and individual force.

This is more pronounced in his staging of works which are more clearly an expression of the naturalism and realism prevalent at the turn of the century. *The Cherry Orchard* and Bertolazzi's *El nost Milan* (*Our Milan*) occupy a significant position in the Strehler canon. They are complementary works: the former a masterpiece of naturalistic drama in a bourgeois setting, the latter a powerful realistic evocation of squalid working-class life. They represent two sides of a coin, in each case requiring the director to bring a whole society to life. In his staging of these two works Strehler has most clearly demonstrated his human and humanitarian interests, presenting the day-to-day lives of individuals tragically trapped in antagonistic social and historical circumstances. Both plays were first mounted – at the Piccolo – in 1955: each was revived to overwhelming critical acclaim two decades later: the former in 1974, the latter in 1979.

The productions of these two works exemplify the distinctive Strehler style, offering insights into his characteristic working methods and serving to define his approach both in the particular context of the Italian stage and within a wider area of theatrical reference. They combine aspects of realism, naturalism, verismo, melodrama and lyricism, aspects which achieved a notable synthesis in the two revivals. The significance of these plays for Strehler is clear, as was the need to return to them after a long period. Dissatisfied with his first version of *The Cherry Orchard*, which suffered from his exhaustion after completing the *Villeggiatura* trilogy, he expressed in 1974 the need 'to do a play I love again and do it better, because it wasn't all there the first time and this has haunted me'. This was an occasion when

sooner or later the interrupted or unfinished dialogue with a play has to be taken up again, either to bring it to an end or simply in order to find out whether or not we ever can bring it to a satisfactory conclusion.[1]

His first attempt at the Bertolazzi was, however, judged both a revelation and a revaluation of the author and his work. Yet he returned to it in 1979, his experience of directing Brecht now allowing him to enrich his insight into the play. In the case of both revivals he has affirmed the *need* to do the play and to do it at that particular time. It is characteristic of his approach that an acknowledged European classic and a virtually unknown work should merit his equal attention and analysis.

The evolution of Strehler's naturalistic style was determined in part by his own cosmopolitan interests in drama and in part by a reaction to the established conventions of the Italian stage. Stanislavski is a crucial reference point in Strehler's approach to acting, which encourages *immedesimazione* (identification with the character) but which takes Brecht's point that it is perfectly justifiable to get into the character providing the performer knows how to get out. The physical clarity of Strehler's work also owes something to Brecht's insistence on the force of the *Gestus*, yet at the same time its sheer bravado owes much to the Italian temperament (one which affected the French performers in his *l'Illusion*). Strehler knows how important the intuitive sense is to the actor; he discusses Eleonora Duse in his conversations with Ronfani, commenting that 'her native intuition made up for any gaps in her theatrical training. She had antennae, she was a great visionary who was able to converse with the spirits', and concluding: 'perhaps she should have worked with a director like Stanislavski. Then we would have had perfection.'[2] His mistrust of the excesses of the *mattatore* is reflected in his admiration for the actor Virgilio Talli, who when he became an actor-manager discovered that 'bringing out the meaning of a play on stage interested him more than acting'.[3] Despite the achievements of Duse and Talli, however, a school of naturalistic acting could never have emerged within the confines of a theatre dominated by the star actor and without the foundation of a permanent company.

Just as Stanislavski's legacy can be seen to have influenced two schools as widely different as the American method and the low-key intellectual naturalism favoured by the British performer, so Strehler's emphasis has a distinctively Italian stamp. It may seem strange that in both the Chekhov and the Bertolazzi dramas actors frequently received noisy and lengthy ovations in the middle of a scene: in the case of *The Cherry Orchard* this is almost inconceivable to a British audience. But Strehler has always assiduously avoided the creation of a 'fourth wall'; as a result he draws the audience into the play and yet offers them a point of critical distance. In this he differs markedly from Visconti, whose stagings – in the late forties and early fifties – of dramas by contemporary American playwrights as well as those of Chekhov had a different naturalistic emphasis. Strehler has explained this as follows:

We had just turned our backs on fake scenery and were getting a reputation for evoking reality through concrete objects, chairs and tables you could touch. Not out of a mere whim or some aesthetic motive – unlike Luchino Visconti, who felt the need to put on stage a real watch, an authentic piece of furniture, or a costume made to measure by a particular tailor. Realism, the conquest of a theatrical reality that you could actually handle physically, was our driving need, an absolute necessity for us;[4]

The fundamental paradox of naturalism is wittily underlined by the critic Alberto Blandi, who commented that in his production of *The Cherry Orchard* Visconti put on show 'a row of authentic – and therefore all the more fake and unconvincing – cherry trees'.[5]

Visconti was a pioneer of cinematic neo-realism, a further point of reference in the context of Italian drama. His early films – *La terra trema*, *Obsession* and *Rocco and his Brothers* – are notable examples of down-to-earth 'slice-of-life' realism in a working-class setting, not without elements of melodrama, both in the sense of a theatrical genre and in relation to lyric opera (or *melodramma*). *El nost Milan* shares all these features – sordid realistic setting, violent larger-than-life plot and a dramatic climax in which the heroine pours out her anger in a long passionate solo (invariably applauded). Moreover, Bertolazzi's play was written in the Milanese dialect of the late nineteenth century. The use of dialect is a feature of the verismo school and its most celebrated exponent, Giovanni Verga. Verga's stories, set among Sicilian peasants, established a vogue for authenticity of language, action and location: in *Cavalleria rusticana*, for instance, which was adapted into the highly successful opera by Mascagni. Strehler's brand of stage naturalism, then, should be seen in the context both of Italian verismo and neo-realism on the one hand, and of Brechtian epic theatre on the other. When he directed the first version of *El nost Milan* he auditioned some 150 actors who specialised in performing dialect plays. His method differed significantly from the tenets of cinematic neo-realism, which insisted on shooting films in genuine locations, employing as performers people taken from the street or factory: amateurs with no stage or screen experience:

The contrast between Strehler's method and that, for example, of De Sica when he shot *Miracle in Milan* serves to clarify the difference between theatrical and cinematic realism. What De Sica did was to search out real-life people and transfer them to a lyrical and imaginative plane; Strehler looked for actors and then transferred them to a plane of realism.[6]

Strehler's approach to *The Cherry Orchard* gives us the clearest idea of his naturalistic method. It was his second production of the Chekhov drama which gave rise to his – now celebrated – theory of the three Chinese boxes, a theory which is particularly appropriate to this play (and author) but which is a significant reference point for his work as a whole. The three boxes function as follows:

In the first box we approach the play on the level of reality: that is to say through the story of a family, its life at a particular moment; in the second we shift to a historical level and in the conflict and struggles of the individual characters we see reflected the social and political conflicts of the period; in the third we are operating in the context of universal – let us call them abstract – values.[7]

In *Per un teatro umano* Strehler explains this in much more detail: in the first instance we are dealing with ordinary human affairs: the buying and selling of a garden, people moving from Paris to Russia and back again; in the second we glimpse a wider panorama of Russia: of the classes which, like Firs, are disappearing or, like Lopakin, getting on; in the third we are aware of the eternal story of human existence, of suffering, resignation, the passage from birth to death. Strehler employs the image of Chinese boxes because each progressive interpretation is a broadening of the perspective, yet the three are interdependent, existing inside 'a fourth box which must contain all three'. The challenge – one triumphantly met by Strehler in the 1974 production – is to realise all three levels of significance in equal depth.

Strehler's achievement in this context can be seen as a fusion of the psychological (or naturalistic), the socio-political (or epic) and the poetic (or lyrical). He draws attention to the dangers of concentrating too closely on any one to the exclusion of the others. Though Stanislavski's production (in 1904) had a lyrical quality, the emphasis was too firmly on the naturalistic, both in terms of setting and characterisation. Too much attention to the significance of the political and historical implications of the play can lead to a tendentiousness which Strehler illustrates by citing the example of a Czech production which, to underline the 'decadence' of Liuba, showed her openly encouraging the servant, Yasha, to caress her legs. The danger of the third approach is one of excessive abstraction, of being out-of-time, bland, neutral;

he cites the Pitoeff production as well as the designs of Svoboda in this context. If the danger inherent in Visconti's 'through the keyhole' type of naturalism is that of losing the wider historical perspective, both the overtly political and the abstract approach have the same defect, of underestimating that quality most important to Strehler: humanity.

He went right to the heart of the matter in 1974 by taking as his starting point the problem of representing the orchard itself. In the 1955 production a branch in blossom had been glimpsed through a window. Strehler now wanted something more pervasive, allusive: 'a curtain of light through which the whole show is seen, a luminous, shifting, impalpable atmosphere, at the same time thick with dust, sun, moon and wind'.[8] In his earliest notes two months before starting rehearsals we find him pondering: 'if a large simple cloth were to extend from the stage into the stalls as though stretched out over the undulating land, giving the impression of hills swaying in the sun (the dark green mountains of Pirandello's giants . . .)'.[9] This materialised as the most striking feature of the production, finally: a thin veil of cloth hung over the stage projecting well into the stalls, it created both a visual and aural effect, having hundreds of (paper) leaves resting on it which rustled and floated down on the audience as it was raised and lowered during the performance. Massimo Gallerani, who assisted on the show, describes it as follows:

This combination of sky and orchard which one minute undulates, seeming to murmur something gentle and tender, then hovers so as to protect the characters before gliding down to caress them, is the basic symbol of the production. This imaginary orchard comprises the audience too as we watch life going by, absorbed by the people who take part in it, wholly aware of our incapacity to change anything.[10]

The strength of the show was in its realisation of issues and ideas in a style which avoided the twin extremes of hyper-naturalism and abstraction. This was the case in Act I, which Strehler observes that Chekhov set in the nursery. This image of the nursery – in Strehler's opinion basic to the meaning of the act and the play as a whole – became a reference point of major significance. 'The director must select certain crucial props to represent the past – objects that *could* be found there and which have the same resonance as the stage directions.'[11] Against a white backcloth the key features of this room assumed a special significance. There were a small table and chairs at which Gaev and Liuba sat playing with a child's tea-service, the school desks at which they had once done their homework, and a large wardrobe which Gaev knocked against as he began his emotive address, whereupon 'in a cloud of dust – the years that have crumbled away – out flew a stream of old toys, coloured balls for the Christmas tree and a child's pram, perhaps the one used by little Grisha, Liuba's dead child'.[12] The theme of a

5   Damiani's set for *The Cherry Orchard,* 1974

return to childhood – reflected most clearly in Liuba's refusal to face reality – pervaded the act and the play. It recurred again with telling force in Act II where Strehler hit on the idea of employing Stanislavski's offstage train in a highly original way. A small train was seen to run across the back of the stage through the undulating hills suggested by the cloth (the carpet of Act I now raised vertically) only to pass across the front of the stage, wobbling on its toy rails. It thus became 'the sign which links the reality of the present both to the future – suggested by the shrill whistle fading away in the distance – and to the past'.[13]

For Strehler Act II is a 'lyrical meditation, an intermezzo, a cantata for many voices within the framework of the four acts'.[14] The musical allusions are significant in a production remarkable for its lyrical power. The notorious stage direction in Act II (which recurs at the end of the play) where Chekhov asks for an offstage sound 'like a string snapping and dying away sadly' was realised by Strehler through a long silence; the characters shuddered and looked around – nothing could be heard – then the veil of cloth trembled and billowed out. The entrance of the tramp immediately after this – speaking in Russian with a slightly drunk but deeply melodious expression – extended the strangeness of the atmosphere, hinting at an unknown ominous future. A further feature of Strehler's sensitivity to sound and to the lyricism of the play – reflected in his citing of Mozart's quintet K.516 as a work of similar clarity and depth – was his orchestration of Act III, which he sees as the clearest example of what Chekhov meant by referring to the play in terms of 'vaudeville'. Here the waltzes, Charlotte's conjuring tricks, the offstage billiards, Trefimov's squabble with Liuba and his comic fall down the stairs were seen as a reflection of life as a game: a game which Liuba tragically loses in this act with the sale of the orchard, a game which Gaev has always played. Strehler observes in his notes that the family has always gambled with the realities of life, a feature which Chekhov tellingly dramatises not through the image of card-playing, but through the far more evocative *aural* effect of the billiards.

The overall design of the production – by Luciano Damiani – reflected the vocal lyricism. Strehler draws attention to a letter of Chekhov's (15 October 1903) in which he wrote: 'Today I finished a play which should prove very entertaining. In it there's a white garden with ladies dressed in white. It's snowing today.' He emphasises that Chekhov was little interested in seeing tree-trunks on stage; rather he wanted 'the vital living presence of this whiteness, of this marvellous white light which could be the light of either summer or winter', and concludes: 'the cherry orchard is both a reality and a symbol'.[15] The abstract white setting dominated by the veil of cloth was peopled with figures dressed in various shades of white: 'clear and brilliant' for Anna, 'pinkish' for Liuba, 'dirty' for Gaev, 'dull' for Varia, 'tired' for Pishkin; only Firs was dressed in black – 'the colour of servants'. The whiteness of the nursery was extended into that of the landscape in Act II and returned with particular force in the final act, where the floorcloth was draped over the furniture before the house was abandoned. In Act III a further aspect of the setting was used to telling effect. The only props on stage were chairs; they took on a special significance for Strehler:

Where does the plastic/symbolic/realistic element reside for the characters in this room? In the chairs. These represent the crucial element that gives the action meaning. They speak volumes: they suggest the idea of property that has been squandered; an empty chair has a hidden, deeper meaning: it is a pointer to the present and the past. A chair on stage represents a most powerful alienation device – there's far more to it than just sitting down. A lot of empty chairs signifies tension, uncertainty, mystery. Who will sit there? Will anyone, ever? What are these chairs waiting for? and for whom? When they are empty they spell loneliness; when occupied, conversation, company, people. People capable of doing anything: making love or dying on them.[16]

Strehler's rehearsal methods are also well documented by Gallerani. The play was rehearsed for ten weeks with a schedule – for the actors – of some eight to nine hours a day. This is entirely characteristic of Strehler's method since his return to the Piccolo in 1972. Gallerani informs us that Strehler encourages the actors to let their own feelings and emotions flow freely in order to give life to the characters. The debt to Stanislavski is more clearly seen in his application of different 'given circumstances' during rehearsal exercises to explore the background of the characters: Franco Graziosi as Lopakin, for instance, was encouraged to explore the potential of this figure as a great lover, hot-tempered, enthusiastic and full of life – in scenes not dramatised by Chekhov. It was Graziosi who in one such exercise suggested that Lopakin once loved Liuba – indeed still does – a feature of the sub-text which was to inform his performance. Strehler is also clear about 'intentions and objectives'. Varia's, for instance, are complex: to marry Lopakin, to marry Anya off to a millionaire, to travel. Her inner frustrations – Strehler explains most convincingly why Lopakin does not propose to her in the crucial scene of Act IV – are vented on objects, as when she continues to rearrange the chairs during her conversation with Epikhodov in Act III. But, as Gallerani points out, Strehler's approach consists of:

a critical application of the Stanislavski method; an alternation between moments when the actors allow their emotions to take over and moments of extreme self-control – with the actors simultaneously sustaining the two extremes. A game of internal versus external reactions, of participation and distancing, of absence and presence.[17]

He cites a particularly striking example in rehearsal: Valentina Cortese's delivery of the long speech about her husband and lover which occurs half-way through Act II:

Tonight Cortese when recounting her past life – downstage right – seemed to me to introduce an aspect of genuinely disturbing madness. The effect is extraordinary, all carried off via this interplay of external and internal emotions; at one moment she seems possessed, the next totally lucid. Then at the height of her emotional recall she suddenly stops, hearing music in the distance . . . Gaev too, but not Lopakin of course.[18]

A markedly similar technical skill – that of shifting constantly between the internal and external life of the character – was evident in Mariangela Melato's performance of Nina in *El nost Milan*. The heroine of this play is much younger than Liuba – in her early twenties; and the role requires immense bravura, culminating in the *pièce de résistance*: the long final speech to her father. In Strehler's revival of the original production, in 1961, the part had in fact been played by Cortese. But Melato, working for the first time with Strehler, scored an individual triumph in the role in 1979. This ability to express a flood of emotion whilst maintaining an objectivity is particularly appropriate to two plays in which the central character alternates between extreme vulnerability and awareness of her folly. In Liuba the two are present throughout the play; in Nina's case the realisation of her error only fully dawns on her to explode in the final scene. Yet throughout the performance – as Renzo Tian remarks – 'Melato makes the part entirely her own, maintaining a remarkable balance between the character's tenderness and her bitter outbursts against life.'[19] The technique exhibited by the leading performer was even more in evidence in the direction. As Giorgio Polacco comments:

This 'appeal to history' which is at the centre of the work is effected through the two fundamentally contrasted techniques of the contemporary theatre: those of Stanislavski and Brecht, of psychological involvement and alienation. Rather than dwelling on this, however, it is more relevant to note how a director – and Strehler is unique in this – has the skill to use each technique to enrich the other, sensitive both to the dramatic style of the play and to its power to accuse, sympathetic to the emotional issues, yet rational and objective.[20]

Bertolazzi's drama is fascinating in the context of Strehler's theory of the Chinese boxes. The different levels of interpretation do not so much overlap here as collide; yet they are all three there and were powerfully realised, most notably in the second production. *El nost Milan* is a vast tapestry in two parts: *La povera gent* (*The Poor*) and *I sciori* (or *The Signori*). Strehler has directed only *La povera gent* (which was first performed in 1893) and in both his versions has concentrated Bertolazzi's four acts into three, combining the central two and giving them one location: 'Ai cusinn economich' – a charitable institution giving food to the poor and unemployed. The first act is set in the Tivoli, a fairground, and the last 'Ai asili notturni', in a public dormitory. Each of these locations is peopled with a different set of low-life and working-class figures who towards the end of the act leave the stage to the three principal figures:

Nina, her father, El Peppon, and her seducer, Togasso. A repeated dramatic pattern thus shows 'slice-of-life' realism giving way to stark melodrama as the story of Nina's seduction and her father's revenge in killing the lover unfolds. In the last act, facing the harsh reality of her existence, Nina tells her father – on his way to give himself up to the police – that she has decided to change her life of poverty and sell the only commodity she has – her youth and beauty – to the *sciori*.

Strehler's achievement – already marked in 1955 and matured by 1979 – was not only to reveal the strengths of a piece which had been out of the repertoire for decades, but to give the play unity and cohesion of style. It was written – and performed – in a late nineteenth-century Milanese dialect difficult even for the present inhabitants of the city to understand; yet the psychological, social and political clarity of the production spoke to Italians and non-Italians alike. In 1955, however, the show was not liked by the majority of French critics when it played in Paris, an event which inspired a long and detailed analysis both of the play and of the production by the semiotician and philosopher Althusser. Through a comparison with the work of Eugène Sue, he pointed out the strength of the piece as residing in an employment of melodrama in order to subvert the ethics which are so often implied in the genre, a feature most forcefully realised in the production:

The powerful conclusion at the end of the play is more than an understanding between Nina and her father: it is the explanation of the difference between a world without illusions and the poor illusions we nurture in our hearts; a confrontation between the real world and that of melodrama which has the effect of destroying all the myths of melodrama.[21]

Althusser further argues that the structure of the drama whereby the issues are brought to a head in the confrontation of the central characters creates a powerful theatrical dialectic which provokes social and political questions. Not insignificantly, the fake world of melodrama finally gives way under what is essentially a Marxist analysis to an awareness of the reality and significance of capital.

Strehler's political concerns are marked in his work on this play. For the revival his reasons for returning to the piece were very different from those which took him back to Chekhov. He felt Bertolazzi's drama was particularly relevant to Milan – to Italy – and to Europe on the verge of the nineteen-eighties. He argues that Milan still has its ghettos, inflation, unemployment, the football pools (a modern equivalent of the lottery which is the one thread of hope to the poor in the second act), commenting:

Rather than resorting to a nostalgic evocation of the period (the play is set in 1890), I felt the need to denounce the reality of our city – our country – our world, object to it in an attempt to change it. We need to ask ourselves painful questions about the future of our co-existence, which we can no longer claim with any certainty is either humane or civilised.[22]

If Strehler's focus was very close to that observed through the perspective characteristic of the second of his Chinese boxes, the day-to-day reality of this world was evoked in a powerfully realistic way which at the same time had a pervasive lyrical quality achieved through the careful organisation of visual and aural rhythms. The opening scene showed a variety of fairground characters looming out of the darkness and talking in subdued furtive tones or shouting barely coherent phrases to one another. From the pitch darkness of the opening, gradually illuminated by the pin-points of lighted cigarettes, a whole world slowly came to life. Nina's search for the clown, Rico, as she peered through the flap of his tent provided another brief source of light which cut across the heavy misty darkness. The refinement of this low-key lighting had the same elusive quality as the carefully orchestrated sounds and actions: the theatrical poetry of this evocation of an unfamiliar, mysterious nocturnal world marked a high point of Strehlerian direction.

These effects were matched by the impressive starkness of the refectory in Act II. As the curtain rose the audience was aware of the clink of spoons against soup-bowls, the only sound which cut across the silence and emptiness of this vast impersonal room with its dominating rear wall bare except for the instructions to the inmates, written across it in large block letters. Two rows of solid wooden benches parallel to the wall and the hatch for dispensing food at right angles to them, stage left, further defined this cold grey space which was shortly to be filled with a cross-section of working-class and unemployed figures. Though recounting individual stories, arguing, joking, or – like the young newly-married couple – mixing their disillusion with their care for one another, these people never come together as a society. We are looking at a picture of immobility and impotence; as Althusser puts it:

You can't close your eyes to the fact that the empty closed cube of this refectory for the poor is a pointer to the time and conditions in which these people are imprisoned.[23]

The complexity of meaning is illustrated by Tian, who describes a significant moment in this act, as observed in the second production:

Details like the entrance of the workmen reduced to automata or the stiff arrogant walk of Togasso, the dandy of the criminal underworld, have the critical force and alienating effect of alarm bells, preventing any sliding into simple naturalism or appeal merely to the emotions. This gives the whole production a dialectical rhythm constantly shifting theatrical focus from slice-of-life realism to a sharply observed critical perspective.[24]

The darkness of Act I and the harsh midday glare of Act II give way to the cold dawn of the final setting. Here the women's gossiping and the persistent rhythm of the clogs as they come and go across the hard floor changes to the powerful tension of the confrontation between Nina and her father. Giorgio Manzini, attending final rehearsals and discussing the work with Strehler, describes how Melato repeated the opening of the monologue at least a dozen times, tearing off her scarf and throwing it to the ground in an attempt to perfect the meaningfulness of this gesture, which is one of anger and revolt, like a whiplash, marking an irrevocable decision. As Nina and her father went their separate ways we were reminded of Nora's slamming of the door in *A Doll's House* as well as of Vivie Warren's rejection of the melodramatic conventions which Shaw has her mother exploit in his drama.

If the starkness of the setting throughout and the emphasis on the need to take a critical stance was influenced by Brecht, the intensity of emotional expression and the truth of the psychological realism in the presentation of both principals and chorus was in tune with Stanislavski. Discussion of these 'three soloists amongst the forty other voices in the chorus of *El nost Milan*' (Gastone Geron in *Il Giornale* (20 December 1979)) underlines the lyrical dimension of the show, in which Nina's final outburst is the culmination of effects from the world of opera, and – in the character and actions of the avenging father – Verdi's *Rigoletto* in particular. That the production should be so rich in dramatic allusion whilst giving these different theatrical genres a powerful and meaningful unity is a measure of Strehler's individual directorial strengths.

3   Goldoni, genius at presenting life

Since even today the bulk of Goldoni critics know absolutely NOTHING about Goldoni, have understood NOTHING, having generalised his work out of existence – his life too, even the *Mémoires* ('Papa Goldoni': who invented this ghastly name?) – then what on earth could his CONTEMPORARIES have made of him?

Goldoni's is a classic case: a tragic, heroic story – low-key perhaps, but still heroic. Goldoni was a person who never compromised . . . right to the bitter end he followed his destiny, his comic genius, his wandering genius, his genius for life. Always watching and evaluating; fascinated, trying to understand: as much as he could, and more.

Strehler, *Per un teatro umano*, p. 93

Shakespeare, Brecht, Goldoni: these are the three dramatists basic to Strehler's theatre. A problem for non-Italians who accept (presumably) the pre-eminence of Shakespeare and (perhaps with less enthusiasm) the significance of Brecht, but remain mystified when brought face to face with Goldoni. The great dramatists Italy has produced – lyric theatre aside (and this is not an aside: the theatrical history of Italy is written in relation to its opera composers) – can be numbered quite literally on the fingers of one hand: they are Goldoni, Pirandello, Dario Fo and Eduardo de Filippo. The limited international fame of Italy's playwrights is out of all proportion to the richness of the country's theatrical tradition. And this should alert us to a very significant fact, one of particular importance in Britain (with a long and distinguished history of playwriting) and America (which has a somewhat shorter but no less impressive history of performance). The strength of Italian theatre resides – has always resided – not in its dramatic literature (indeed the phrase reverberates with the contradictions which are currently tearing the academic institutions of Italy apart) but in its cunning assimilation and combination of theatrical skills. The writer, the director, the actor, the audience all assume positions of comparable significance in a theatre which employs simultaneously all the available means of communication.

The particular power of Italian theatre resides in this openness, this roughness (to employ a word dear to Peter Brook), this awareness of its place in a social and historical context. The howls of laughter which greet Dario Fo's inspired clowning; the adoration which can make Eduardo de Filippo a life senator in the Italian parliament; the sound of two thousand people congratulating with their bravos the sublime artistry of Pavarotti; the fact that the region of Emilia Romagna can write off a debt for a Luca Ronconi production (in 1988) which ran a million pounds over budget (and this was for a play – *Il dialogo delle carmelitane* – not an opera): all these give some indication of the relative significance of the writer in Italian theatre. In a country such as Britain, dominated by the importance and power of the playwright, where the art of the director is overshadowed by that of the actor (or even the designer), where lyric opera is considered the entertainment of a wealthy elite and where there is absolutely no relationship between a popular culture and a sophisticated political dialectic, the art of Goldoni – and its significance to Strehler – must appear a mystery.

Goldoni must be read – and seen – in the context of popular theatre, in the context of political theatre (Strehler's insistence on the affinities between his work and that of Brecht is fundamental) and in the particular context of Italian drama, which – outside the field of lyric opera – has always had an uphill struggle in establishing its credentials. Goldoni is no longer a popular dramatist, even in Italy. Only a few of his plays are regularly performed (a playwright writing essentially in Venetian dialect of the mid eighteenth century has a severely limited currency in the age of television); but he does remain a crucial point of focus for Italian theatre. His literary reputation and the stage history of his plays are not entirely complementary, though the same prejudices and opinions have influenced both spheres; Strehler's productions have been in large part responsible for a major revaluation of Goldoni's work in Italy and abroad.

The National Theatre in London has undertaken two Goldoni productions, *Il campiello* and the *Villeggiatura* trilogy. Neither was much of a success. Goldoni's art does not easily transfer to an Anglo-Saxon context. *Il campiello* (*The Little Square*) and the *Villeggiatura* trilogy, though written within five years of one another, represent opposite poles in Goldoni's creative writing. Is it a coincidence that the National Theatre chose these two productions, amongst the most celebrated of Strehler's shows? *Il campiello* (Strehler's last production of a new Goldoni play to date) celebrates and examines the life of the people who inhabit a small square in Venice and their relationship with three outsiders; there is a fascinating clash of social (and political) values between the people who live and work in the square and those whose lifestyle effectively excludes them from the social life of the campiello. This is one of Goldoni's few working-class comedies and, written as it was by a member of the middle class shortly before the French Revolution, it represents a complex document. More complex, indeed, as Strehler's production revealed, than his masterpiece, *Le baruffe chiozzotte* (*The Squabbles at Chioggia*), a picture of a small fishing community which was to explode on the stage of the Piccolo Teatro (and then on scores of others in a long tour) in 1964. The fact that *Il campiello* is written in (complex) verse and set in a small

Venetian square counted for little in the National Theatre production, which transferred the setting to Scotland. Strehler's Brechtian point of view, his love for the society presented and his obsessive concern for the language of the piece (a challenge on account of both the eighteenth-century Venetian dialogue and the subtle verse structure) made for a very different impact on the Italian stage.

No less successful and significant was his production of the *Villeggiatura* trilogy in 1954, a work to which he has returned and which is particularly significant in his exploration of Goldoni, not least because his wife, Andrea Jonasson, played the central role in the Vienna revival of 1974. Strehler was the first director to offer the three plays of this trilogy as a single and composite entertainment in one evening. They are still – and always were meant to be – performed separately (they are three full-length plays), but they are clearly interrelated and by judicious cutting – not entirely dissimilar to that in the Barton–Hall adaptation of the three parts of Shakespeare's *Henry VI* – Strehler reduced the trilogy to a (long) single evening's entertainment. The trilogy represents Goldoni's career at the very end of his work in Venice. Strehler saw its characters through the eyes of their creator and through his own: those of a director conscious of a particular period of history (shortly before the French Revolution) when the values of a bourgeois society were in crisis. Again, this was not the viewpoint of the National Theatre production or of the critics and public, who find – and this is a major stumbling-block in the way of Goldoni's acceptance in Britain – an uncomfortable parallel with the English comedy of manners. English literary critics are unable to appreciate that there is a world of difference between – on the one hand – the concerns and styles of Goldoni and – on the other – those of either his contemporaries Sheridan and Goldsmith or earlier dramatists such as Wycherley who, writing as they too were in a period of revolutionary political and social change, are in a truer sense much closer to Goldoni. But the latter are closer only in their political and social sensibility. Their awareness parallels that of Goldoni (as that of Sheridan and Goldsmith undoubtedly does not) but the savagery of their satirical observation, expressed through a consummate command of language, finds no equivalent in the Italian dramatist. Hence the British problem of finding Goldoni lacking in wit, a sort of poor Italian relation of Molière.

Any in-depth research into Goldoni's theatre requires an understanding of the commedia dell'arte. Commedia has fascinated Strehler throughout his career and his revitalisation of the genre is evident in pieces as different as *The Tempest*, Corneille's *L'Illusion* and *Don Giovanni*. Commedia can be traced back to the ancient Roman theatre but it was in the early sixteenth century that the style and techniques used by later artists crystallised. The literal meaning of commedia dell'arte implies comedy performed by professionals, actors able to take a scenario and improvise dialogue whilst introducing *lazzi* (comic pieces of business) which tested their wit and physical ingenuity. The drama revolved round a set group of figures: a pair of lovers, two old men and a series of comic servants or clowns. Pantalone – usually the father of the heroine – is a foolish old man in contrast to the pedantic lawyer, Il Dottore. There are essentially three families (or types) of clown: Arlecchino, the poor servant, ever resourceful, but often out of his depth; Brighella, a more sinister, conniving figure; and Pulcinella, the tragi-comic victim. By the eighteenth century (indeed well before) commedia had lost much of its vitality: improvisatory skills had declined, the language had become banal and the *lazzi* had degenerated into stock routines. Goldoni's celebrated 'reform' consisted in breathing new life into the stock characters by giving them fresh conversation, placing them in a recognisable social context and providing a new edge to the plot and situation. He was opposed by the aristocrat Count Carlo Gozzi, who felt Goldoni had vulgarised the genre (by creating sympathetic portraits of servants whilst satirising their masters) and who held the essence of commedia to be improvisation.

Arlecchino or *The Servant of Two Masters*, one of Goldoni's earliest dramas (written in 1745), exploits all the features detailed above. Clarice, the daughter of Pantalone, loves Silvio, the son of Doctor Lombardi. The fathers encourage the match when they hear the man to whom she has been promised – Federigo Rasponi – has been killed in a duel. Their plan encounters difficulties when Federigo appears, claiming he was merely wounded. This is not in fact Federigo but his sister Beatrice in disguise. She is searching for her lover, Florindo, the very man who has killed her brother. When Florindo himself arrives in Venice he engages Arlecchino as a servant, unaware that he is already working for Beatrice. The situation is ripe for a sequence of misunderstandings compounded by Arlecchino, who, in a desperate attempt to sustain his dual role, is ultimately obliged to serve a meal to his two masters simultaneously as they lodge in adjoining rooms at the same inn.

This drama has dominated Strehler's theatre. It formed part of the Piccolo's first season in 1947 and it has remained in the repertoire ever since, a point of reference for the whole of Strehler's work. Though in forty years only two actors have played the role of Arlecchino, Strehler has undertaken six different productions of the work, each a continuation and development of the one before. From a rather generalised exercise in commedia dell'arte, the play has become the key to the company's style and an ever-changing index of its condition. It is the play which has been most consistently toured in Italy and abroad, the one which is regarded as the particular property of the Piccolo.

What has led Strehler to undertake no less than six productions of the play and to make sure that it has never for long been out of the repertoire? In answering these questions we not only appreciate the particular significance of this play for Italians in general and Strehler in particular, but are also able to observe the development and the enriching of Strehler's directorial gifts. Let us first of all give a rapid survey of the play's production history at the Piccolo. In 1947 – as the last of four plays presented in the first season – it was performed more as a tribute to a particular style, the commedia dell'arte, than as an interpretation of Goldoni. The point of reference here was Reinhardt, whose production twenty years previously encouraged Strehler to an exercise in the mechanical fascination of the genre: its dexterity and cleverness *per se*. In 1952 Strehler undertook another production in which for the first time he introduced comic *lazzi* from the general commedia repertoire. He substantially changed not only the written text (which was treated more as a scenario) but the overall piece, which, as the critic Luigi Lunari has pointed out, 'changed from within, resulting in a total transformation of the work'[1]. This version, fortuitously, was filmed and it remains a treasure-trove for the researcher. In 1956 the implications opened up by this dramatically new staging were taken an inevitable degree further and a whole new dimension added. The audience observed not only the Goldoni play but a sort of 'play-*outside*-a-play' in which the performers, once they had completed a scene, had another, equally fascinating life. They did not disappear into the wings, they merely came off the raised platform on which they were performing the Goldoni and were seen in a different offstage life: discussing, arguing, flirting, going about their day-to-day routine. Through this device – which we will discuss in more detail later – Strehler was able to give the work a new life by opening up a possibility for improvisation which lay behind the original play but which had been avoided in the first (1947) staging and too severely programmed in the second (1952).

The play – for many critics – assumed its definitive form in the fourth version, first performed in the Villa Litta at Affori (in the open air) in the summer of 1963. On this occasion the offstage life of the actors was given even fuller expression as the significance of the small platform on which *Arlecchino* was performed shrank whilst the rest of the stage space was taken up by two large carts, the homes of two families who made up the company. The actors invented – through improvisation – a whole life for the 'second' character they were representing: the interpreter of the role in the Goldoni original. This version remained in the repertoire for a relatively long period – until 1977, when Strehler did an entirely different (fifth) production, first seen at the Odéon in Paris. The company performing *Arlecchino* were still in evidence in their offstage life but now they had grown older and tired. Instead of taking place in the open air in front of a villa (whose owner clearly cared for the company), the play was now being performed indoors – in a large empty room, dominated by a broken-down equestrian statue. The atmosphere was dark, literally in terms of the lighting, but more particularly so in the sense of weariness and melancholy which suffused the production. This remained in the repertoire until 1987, the fortieth anniversary of the Piccolo, when Strehler produced yet another – very different – version, a valedictory one, entitled 'l'edizione dell'addio'. This managed to sum up and combine features from all the others. It was rigorously simple – no set, no stage-within-a stage, merely a grey floor and backcloth, and three screens illuminated by a series of portable candelabra. Instead of the brooding gloomy quality of the previous production this one had all the verve and freshness of a Venetian carnival night: the action was fast, the cast apparently rejuvenated. There was no longer a play-within-a-play, but the residue of previous productions was felt in the presence of an elderly prompter (who gave the signal to begin each act) as well as in some of the direct addresses to the audience. The work seemed at once age-old and brand new.

Let us examine these productions in more detail. That first production (1947) revealed – according to Lunari – 'an interest not so much in Goldoni as in the pre-Goldonian style of the commedia dell'arte; this was in line with a particular middle-European emphasis (which has its origins in the critical attitudes of Schiller and Schlegel) which sees Goldoni essentially as suffocating the commedia tradition in his insistence on a type of flat bourgeois realism, and which has always preferred the original commedia or the use to which Carlo Gozzi put it rather than the work of Goldoni'.[2] This may seem a strange observation to make about a man who has championed the work of Goldoni and placed his drama on the same level as that of Shakespeare and Brecht, but Strehler is not in disagreement with Lunari. His point of reference was Reinhardt, and this first production was not concerned with the historical context of the piece, exploring instead its fascination as a type of 'abstract theatrical machine'. Strehler was particularly hard on the actors in this show, forcing them to wear masks which were clumsily made and very uncomfortable. Created out of stiff cardboard and lint, they pressed into the skin, constricted the eyelashes and by the end of each show, because of the excessive perspiration, were inevitably reduced to shreds.

The masks were uncomfortable in two senses: the physical and the psychological. Marcello Moretti, Strehler's first – great – Arlecchino, resolved the problem crudely by refusing to wear the mask and painting one on his face instead. The way in which he gradually came to 'accept the tyranny of the mask' – as Strehler puts it – sheds a wealth of light on the implications of this show in particular and the tradition of commedia in general. 'The mask', says Strehler, 'is a mysterious and terrible instrument . . .

it brings us to the very threshold of theatrical mystery, demons are reborn through these immutable, immobile, static faces'.[3] The mask denies any possibility of a concrete realistic gesture and forces the actor to discover a whole new physical vocabulary with his entire body. It also places deep psychological strain on the performer. Only when skilful flexible masks designed in leather by Amleto Sartori were employed in the second production of *Arlecchino* did Moretti accept these implications. He experimented with a series of masks representing animal types, preferring at first the cat mask but moving through one resembling a wolf to one (which became definitive) characteristic of the *zanni*, the ridiculous comic servant. Strehler points out that Moretti was the first to discover the endless mobility of the mask: he realised the full expressive force of its mouth and gradually discovered how to externalise a whole range of emotions when he let himself be 'conquered' by the mask; he found liberty in the restriction, and the most rigid of conventions released his imaginative capacity, allowing him to realise the most vital part of himself. Strehler comments: 'behind the mask, Marcello, who was shy (like all actors and he more than most), was able to release a new life, an imaginative power which was in no way "realistic" but securely anchored in his own down-to-earth inner self, and carry through that process of rediscovery and enrichment which I myself was undertaking from my own point of view into the problem of commedia dell'arte, which seemed to have been miraculously reborn before our very eyes'.[4]

The second production marked the beginnings of that exploration of the Goldoni play which was to open up more and more complex avenues of interpretation. It was set very precisely in the eighteenth century; the costumes were authentic and the setting (very simple, with cloth backdrops which were drawn aside to change the scenes) gave the impression of a staging by travelling players of the period. The great innovation was the introduction of the comic *lazzi* and the consequent enriching of the play's texture. The scene in which Arlecchino manages to serve dinner to both his 'masters' simultaneously, which marks the height of comic ingenuity in the play, was distinguished by the balletic verve of Moretti and the addition of endless gags. Moretti entered performing an extraordinary balancing act with a soup tureen, crawling in on his back, moving onto all fours before finally standing with the tureen. The whole scene was danced: he executed a powerful échappé to kick one of the waiters off the stage and performed a perfect pirouette before taking the jelly. This prop had a life of its own: it was slapped soundly, admired, and put on the ground only to follow Arlecchino obediently offstage at the end of the scene. From the fairly straightforward stage directions of the original Strehler built up a whole complex ballet culminating in Arlecchino rushing madly from one side of the stage to the other, frantically catching the fresh dishes and throwing the dirty ones to the waiters who appear and disappear continuously from the upstage doors.

Even more intriguing, however, because more reliant on inspired improvisation, is the scene in which Arlecchino attempts to reseal the letter addressed to Beatrice which has been opened by her lover, Florindo. Moretti begins by lying flat on the floor, gazing at the letter from different angles and then attempts to fold it whilst it floats out of his reach. He remembers that his grandmother used a trick of employing half-chewed bread to reseal a letter. He unwinds an (endlessly long) piece of cloth in which he keeps the bread but as he attempts to moisten each small piece hunger forces him to eat them. The solution is the production of a final piece of bread tied to length of string which he hangs on to with one hand. His methods of pressing the letter constitute a delirious catalogue of comic effects. He cannot stamp on the letter as this would dirty it; he tries to press it with his head whilst executing a nimble handstand; and finally hits on the expedient of sitting on the letter. But it sticks to his bottom and, in terror that he has lost it, he appeals desperately to the audience – now helpless with laughter – to tell him where it is.

As any director or performer knows, nothing stales as quickly as improvisation, whether verbal or physical; and it was this realisation during the run of the second production of *Arlecchino* which led Strehler to the ingenious and original expedient of inventing offstage lives for his players in succeeding productions. This allowed him simultaneously to retain the pace of the Goldoni play and provide the actors with a means of keeping their performances fresh through improvisation in the interpolated sequences. In the second (1952) production the actor playing Silvio employed a very funny gag when making the grand gesture of threatening the disguised Beatrice under the assumption that she is Frederico. In the original text he states, 'The man who wants to marry Clarice will have to reckon with this sword', and – drawing it – leaves. In the Strehler production a repeated gag showed the sword refusing to budge from the scabbard with the result that Silvio was obliged to repeat the phrase 'with this sword' several times, each to more risible effect, and finally exit saying: 'with another sword'. Such a gag has a limited life in the theatre, and a large measure of the fascination of Strehler's various stagings of this play resides in the acute awareness of how and when creative innovation born of improvisation and experiment can in turn become a dead cliché. In his development of this issue through the different productions of *Arlecchino* he reveals a profound understanding of the acting profession itself, a paradox basic to Goldoni's own attempts at theatrical reform.

The third production (1956) saw the emergence of the definitive form the play was thereafter to take in three successive versions. Ezio Frigerio's set limited the stage-within-a-stage to four square metres – a small wooden construction, a little lower than the type used by travelling commedia actors in the sixteenth and seventeenth centuries – and employed detailed backcloths run on wires to represent the three basic locations. Pantalone's house was opulent and grandiose with Bibiena-style columns, majestic portals and frescoes and a plethora of black and white marble. The area outside Brighella's locanda was clearly a Venetian 'calle', or narrow street, not a square. In the foreground baroque architecture could be glimpsed with small balconies in the background leading to a perspective with a view of San Salute. The room in the locanda was no undefined annexe but the kitchen itself, with plates, dishes and culinary equipment painted with the same meticulous detail on the backcloth.

This clearly defined stage area was in contrast to the crumbling walls of the villa or palace glimpsed in the background with its pieces of masonry and fallen columns adding to the gloomy atmosphere. Above the booth stage were hung three long strips of thin material gathered in folds, running back from the proscenium. As one critic has remarked, they suggested 'the swollen sails of a ship, the mobility of a travelling show (since touring actors needed protection from the sun), the cloth stretched over the windows of some Mediterranean villa or the material depicting a Louis XVIII salon'.[5]

As soon as the actors had finished their scenes they came off the small stage, took off their masks, watched the action that followed, scrutinized the reactions of the audience, had a swig of wine, chatted with a colleague, prepared for their next entrance. Here was the initial outline of what was to become a much more elaborate superstructure in the next production (1963). Gradually, as these two related productions developed, the audience stopped being interested in Beatrice's story, Clarice's situation or Arlecchino's daring *for their own sake*; as Lunari puts it: 'What became important was the *style* of performance, the technique of the actors, the comic invention, the virtuosity in the delivery of the quick-patter dialogue; the relationship between the characters was no longer the point of interest, it was the relationship between the performers; the *plot* itself was not central, but rather the *theatrical style* employed to narrate it.'[6]

Moreover, with the fuller development of the contrast between traditional play and novel invention the production became: 'not merely the story of a company of commedia actors but also the story of a show, which has developed via the theatrical devices which – from one version to the next – have accompanied it in its journey from one place to another: it has remained the same show, evolving, however, through its constantly-changing central features'.[7] The prompt book of the 1963 version gives us a vivid impression of the extent to which the show had become highly original and complex.

There is a lengthy prologue which sets the situation and indicates how it will develop through the production as a whole:

Two large carts stand in a field. The horses have been unbridled and led off. Two little wooden ladders convert the carts into two small houses which face one another some ten yards apart. Between them the actors, who have come off the carts, have put up the stage: a sort of square platform, bounded on one side by the metal shades for the candles which form the footlights, and on the other by two wooden supports and a bar with runs for the backdrops: representing an alleyway, a room in Pantalone's house, the interior of an inn etc. Between the platform stage and the carts are a variety of props used in different shows: drums, kings' helmets and queens' robes for tragedy, masks for comedy, a papier-mâché chicken, a trophy, an Inca idol for some play or other about Cortez. And behind the stage two tables with all the necessary props for the evenings performance. Further away, by the two respective carts, two banners — something between a travelling minstrel's standard and the sacred image carried in a procession — are waving in the breeze. They show Arlecchino and Brighella respectively, dimly lit by the flames of the two torches. The actors move between the carts, the stage and the various props entering from and exiting into the big house, a villa in front of which they have erected their travelling stage. The owner of the house — a nobleman or wealthy merchant, probably — has courteously allowed them to use a couple of rooms on the ground floor, where they can refresh themselves with the odd glass of wine. The audience is assembling. The sun has set: the first shadows of the evening are falling.

The scene comes to life as the performance is about to start: we now hear an actor's voice in the distance. And the sound of a bell which the stage manager is ringing as he moves between the carts, the stage and the props. He goes up to the villa to give the actors their call and warn them the show is about to begin.[8]

These lengthy stage directions are followed by an extended (three-page) scene in which we are introduced to the company and given clear impressions of the relationships between the players. The actor playing Doctor Lombardi does some voice exercises, the prompter brings on his stool, the actor playing Pantalone rehearses a new piece of business with the actor playing Silvio. They continue to improvise as the actress playing Smeraldina empties a bucket of water, soaking the boots of the actor playing Florindo. The Doctor rehearses the lower register of his voice, fails to impress Brighella and the two argue about upstaging. The show begins with the actors bowing first to one another and then to the audience whilst a young inexperienced member of the company ('perhaps the son of the actor playing Doctor Lombardi', the stage directions suggest) is encouraged to overcome his shyness and give the official start to the show proper by banging on the stage with a heavy stick. As the play developed it became clear that each of Strehler's performers had worked out a complex personal history for the eighteenth-century actor he was presenting. Gradually a story emerged of two rival families of actors within the same company with the two eldest and most experienced actors (those playing the Doctor and Pantalone) as their respective leaders, endlessly engaged in making the most of their own group's potential on stage and stealing effects whenever possible from the other. A particularly striking moment was that in which one of the porters (a small role) went off after a comic scene, threw a look of real hatred at the actors still on stage, before making a slow brooding exit. No explanation was given: the moment was all the more striking for its element of mystery.

The part of Pantalone in the first three productions was played by Antonio Battistella, and in a diary he kept of the 1956 tour there is an extension of the Pirandellian fascination with the on-stage and off-stage lives of the actors basic to Strehler's third and subsequent versions. From the pages of this diary the life of a company of Italian actors subjected to the rigours of a Northern tour (which took in Britain, Scandinavia and Germany) emerges with amusing – at times touching – clarity. There were within the company itself all the types so familiar from Pirandello's *Six Characters* or Goldoni's dramas. There is the prima donna – Giusi Dandolo – whose affectations are amusingly related by Battistella, notably a 'scena' she elaborates to explain her lack of a passport through the 'truly incomprehensible obstruction on the part of the relevant authorities. Her attempt,' he explains, 'to narrate her misadventures, over-dramatising the whole issue, fell on the stony ground of unanimous indifference.' He narrates the ups-and-downs in the relationship of two 'innamorati' in the company who are more interested in one another than in the production and who spend a somewhat frustrating honeymoon night in separate compartments on the train from Milan. An amusing picture emerges of Paolo Grassi's eating habits (and unsuccessful attempts to diet); on one occasion, when he said he had no appetite at all – Battistella tells us – the distinguished artistic director 'made do with smoked salmon, a couple of boiled eggs, a piece of meat, three salads, a few prawns and nineteen buttered rolls'.[9]

Battistella was not the Pantalone of the fourth production; nor – more significantly – was Moretti the Arlecchino: he died tragically in January 1961. The role passed to Ferruccio Soleri who had, fortuitously, been coached by Moretti when the Americans insisted on an understudy during the tour there in 1960. In one of Strehler's most revealing passages in *Per un teatro umano* he discusses the procedure whereby the younger actor was initiated into the mystery and craft of creating this role. What he has to say is particularly significant in our understanding both of the way Strehler works and of how a vital tradition can be learnt and thus perpetuated. 'How is it possible not to have in mind the "continuity" of theatre', Strehler asks, 'the evolution of theatrical generations, the patrimony of experience which is handed down over the years? By a miracle', he goes on, 'in the midst of the present day we were witnesses to a live process which was characteristic of the commedia dell'arte; of commedia, that is, as the profession of the comic actor. A profession which one commedia actor inherits from another, with all the enriching that implies.' He describes Moretti's way of teaching his young pupil: quite lacking in formal methodical training, based on experience with a mixture of very personal illustrative gestures and a smattering of theory.

It was as though I were present at a mysterious ritual whose aim and method were far from clear . . . Marcello watched this new Arlecchino grow, day by day: shy, uncertain, following precisely in his footsteps, recreating his tone of voice and movements, though here and there, quite naturally, there appeared traces of a new Arlecchino, different from his own. And he would watch him with a very complex mixture of feelings, part love, part rejection, part indifference, part defence. I had the impression of a strangely maternal sort of love, containing its share of jealousy and anxiety. The young Arlecchino (Ferruccio Soleri) had even begun, little by little, to pick up some of Moretti's rehearsal mannerisms: after one scene he'd be wearing a big towel round his neck, and after the scene in which he serves the two meals he'd even have a second towel round his face. Wrapped up like this the two Arlecchini moved around the empty stage during pauses in the rehearsals. Ours is such a closed-off world, on the outskirts of life, and the lore of the actor ends up being nothing more than a string of anecdotes, memories, the recounting of data. Perhaps precisely because these few facts are the only concrete thing to hang on to in our profession; anything else, the key or secret, can't be explained to anyone. The tenderness of these two Arlecchini, brought together in this way by a particular necessity, needs no explanation. It gives a concrete impression of what is most human and humane about our profession: brotherhood, caring for one another . . . The most beautiful memory Marcello Moretti has left me is this. I want this final gesture of his to be the one that stays with me right to the end: that of giving something profound and precious of himself to someone else. So that the theatre might continue in this dark age to help men to live with one another.[10]

Strehler's six productions, then, neatly divide between the first three, starring Moretti, and the last three, starring Soleri (who has now been playing the title role for nearly thirty years).

Gianfranco Mauri has been playing the part of Brighella for almost as long, in fact. It was Mauri who in an inspired improvisation during the last production (now, of course, a permanent feature of the show) came out of character and offstage in the scene when Beatrice is explaining to him how she expects to receive letters both under her real name and her assumed one – a particularly convoluted turn of the plot – to announce that he had been playing the role for thirty-two years and he still couldn't understand this twist of the story. It is a further example of the meta-theatrical game Strehler has been playing with this piece for over thirty years; and it is intriguing that he has now reached a point where he can dispense with the Pirandellian device of the play-within-a-play entirely.

This final staging (1987) restored the balance to a production which several critics felt had grown too dark, emphasising the passing of the years and the significance of this for the performers all too strongly. The atmosphere of desolation created by the setting in the fifth version (1977, at the Odéon, Paris) suffused the whole piece with a feeling that here was a company that was tired, struggling bravely at the end of a tradition. 'An air of melancholy, of decadence almost . . . the noble inhabitants of the palace are not to be seen, nor their presence felt; yet their absence is both tangible and significant, the sign that something has changed or is changing. Compared to the hospitality and good will of the nobility who supported the *Arlecchino* at the Villa Litta, the new owners in whose house the show is taking place give the impression of having more important things to think about.'[11]

The company in the final production are free of any such patronage. Their show appears to be taking place on the side of the lagoon, as the candelabra placed next to the backdrop give the impression of lights reflected in the water. In his conversation with Ugo Ronfani (published in 1986) Strehler had already expressed the wish to direct an *Arlecchino* set on the wooden jetty in Chioggia: the point at which the fisherman arrive in *Le baruffe chiozzotte*. This is the atmosphere suggested by his final version of the play, which (like the previous one) has a nocturnal setting. Here, however, the story unfolds in a blaze of light and with an energy on the part of the performers which banishes the shadows and cobwebs of the previous production, reinstating the life-enhancing vitality of both the play and the commedia tradition.

The development of Strehler's *Arlecchino* is most marked in the contrast between the stage settings of the third (1956) production and the last (in 1987). Coming two years after the *Villeggiatura* trilogy, the same year as *The Threepenny Opera*, the 1956 production was strong in historical and social detail, whilst at the same time exploiting to the full the meta-theatrical implications of the work in the observation of the actors both on and off the stage. The three basic features of the Ezio Frigerio's set – the booth stage (with its detailed backcloths), the ruined walls and the three suspended drapes – served to crystallise the production's central preoccupation: 'Three areas of focus in this new setting: the present – the play, here and now, full of fun and laughter; the past, evoking sadness and nostalgia; and then finally the impassive universe implying future promise'.[12]

The semiology of the stage space – again designed by Frigerio – was very different in the final production. As Ugo Ronfani states:

Strehler has proceeded here by subtraction, eliminating just about all the stage signs and entrusting any definition of the setting to the utterances of an old-style prompter; the space is furnished with only three screens, two small tables and candelabra . . . Everything hangs on the rhythm (since the challenge was to demonstrate the irrepressible youthfulness of a veteran company) – Strehler has enriched the intrigues and effectively 'anthologised' the comic effects accumulated in forty years of research.[13]

Even more than Strehler's *Lear* staging, this Goldoni production was 'the thing itself':

Venice? A bare stage with a misty backcloth (plus the flames of the Maghera refineries). Pantalone's house? Two valets carrying candelabra. Brighella's locanda? Plates and omelettes hurled behind whirling screens.[14]

Strehler was able to distil even more meaning from a staging which in its abstract purity was at the furthest extreme from the detailed complexity of the 1956 version. It was the lighting in this instance which gave the show subtlety and depth of meaning:

The mystery is dependent on the magic of the lights – the flames of the candles serving as footlights, the suggestion of noonday heat or moonlight reflected in the transparent backcloth, the candelabra carried by the valets: all taking place on bare planks – a down-to-earth ritual. In contrast to the severity of the empty stage the phantasmagoric costumes of Franca Squarciapino acquire a mythic significance which accentuates the dreamlike projection of a tale no longer contrasting characters and masks, but reality and illusion.[15]

If this gradually evolving *Arlecchino* has defined one aspect of his progress as a director – making its presence felt outside the Goldoni canon in works as different as *The Tempest*, Corneille's *L'Illusion* and Mozart's *Don Giovanni* – another aspect of his approach to Goldoni is equally clear and significant. Lunari has pointed out that in several major respects Strehler's choice of Goldoni plays has mirrored the development in the playwright himself from a concern with the specific problems of commedia through those basic to his theatrical reform to a critique of bourgeois life and a celebration of the working-class community. This is a simplification but it is worth considering. With the second *Arlecchino* production Strehler began his investigation into the paradoxes of the commedia genre. One aspect of Goldoni's reform was the placing of the traditional figures in a recognisable everyday setting in which they carry out their roles as servants, masters, lovers and so forth within the context of a realistic and coherent story. Strehler's productions of *La putta onorata* (*The Good Girl*) (1950), *L'amante militare* (*The Army Lover*) (1952) and *La vedova scaltra* (*The Artful Widow*) (1953) explore this area of Goldoni. With the *Villeggiatura* trilogy – first produced in 1954 at the Piccolo, then again in Vienna (at the Burgtheater in 1974) and once more with the Comédie-Française in Paris (at the Odéon in 1979) – he undertook a critical survey of that middle-class world which in the earlier plays is the subject of Goldoni's more familiar good humour. In 1964 and 1975 respectively Strehler directed Goldoni's two masterpieces of working-class life, *Il campiello* and *Le baruffe chiozzotte*, which represent challenges – in terms of setting, acting conventions and audience response – of a very different order.

Had Strehler undertaken no other productions of *Arlecchino*, his first staging might have been relegated to the theatrical archive, as have the other plays of that first 1947 season. His subsequent Goldoni productions did not meet with unanimous critical approval until he undertook the *Villeggiatura* trilogy in1954. This alerted the Italians (and the world) to the fact that here was a director capable of revealing the mastery of this so often underestimated Italian dramatist. The critics wrote unanimously of the 'modernity' of Goldoni; of the fact that the characters spoke with the voices of present-day people. Strehler has made Goldoni an endlessly relevant, ever-entertaining dramatist, but did not achieve this until his productions of the *Villeggiatura* trilogy. Was this because of the nature of the plays? his own immaturity as a director? the difficulties of interpreting Goldoni for a modern audience? It was undoubtedly a combination of all three: they go together, and it is a measure of Strehler's skill as a director that he has worked his way very gradually – and carefully – into the Goldoni canon.

It is interesting to take note at this point of his production of *Gli innamorati* (*The Lovers*) (1950). This play (and production) falls outside the neat schema suggested by Lunari, since it is effectively contemporary with the *Villeggiatura* trilogy and just before *Le baruffe chiozzotte*. It is the only one of the plays undertaken by Strehler in the period between *Arlecchino* and the *Villeggiatura* trilogy which does not employ the stock commedia characters; we are in the bourgeois world of the comedy of manners. The production was not liked. Dino Buzzati began his review by asking how Strehler would direct this piece. The critics were already familiar with his *Arlecchino* and they had seen (earlier that year) *La putta onorata*. 'Well, well – one of my friends said – I'm looking forward to seeing what Strehler makes of *Gli innamorati*. There isn't much leaping about in this play. No bowing and scraping, pirouettes or ballet. Just talk, Nothing else . . .' Buzzati ended his review by saying that this production had wit, intelligence and harmony but he was bothered by the (for him) exaggerated 'bleating' of Fulgenzio.[16] Eligio Possenti most clearly summed up what was considered to be the fault of the production: an exaggeration in the characterisation which did not conform to the traditional stylisation felt to be appropriate for playing Goldoni. Strehler was criticised for having too little respect for eighteenth-century manners and conventions, distorting the work with his original psychological emphasis:

The farcical tone is excessive, inappropriate to this limpid, harmonious comedy. He all too often replaces grace with affectation, presenting us with an edgy modern approach in place of the jovial satire of the original.[17]

Strehler had already begun his critique of that area of bourgeois behaviour which was to find its much richer expression four years later in his *Villeggiatura*. It is worth noting Gastone Geron's comment that we must take into account the response of an audience 'still tied to the criteria of an out-of-date pseudo-naturalistic style and too familiar with the soggy distortions familiar from sugary sentimental interpretations'.[18] In short, Strehler was already undertaking a revaluation of the Goldoni repertoire, even if he was not – at this point – fully capable of overturning the traditional tables.

The production of *La putta onorata* in the same year (1950) met with even less success. It was performed in the open air, in the Campo San Trovaso in Venice, and this was not felt to be advantageous. The critics could speak here of Strehler choosing a 'minor' Goldoni: something different from the usual plays performed under such circumstances. This is the most revealing comment of all. *L'amante militare* – performed in a double bill with Molière's *Le Médecin volant* (*The Flying Doctor*) – in 1952 met with much greater critical success. Here was an (acknowledged) minor work which was critically rediscovered with all the force that greeted Clifford Williams's production of the *The Comedy of Errors* at the RSC in 1962. (Indeed Philip Hope-Wallace, reviewing the Strehler *Arlecchino* at the Aldwych in May 1967, referred to its influence on the *Comedy of Errors* and commented on the 'fertile effect on production generally throughout Europe of the Strehler show'.) Arlecchino features in *L'amante militare* and the role was (of course) played by Moretti. Strehler had already begun to experiment with his improvisations on a Goldoni text in this production, which predates – by six months – the second version of *Arlecchino*. It delighted the critics, as the comments of Raffaele Carriere make clear: 'I prefer Strehler when he makes a work of art out of nothing. When he leaves the worthy classics alone and concerns himself with the hurried scenario (albeit of a genius). Because without Strehler what would this comedy at the Piccolo have been? . . . Spanish officers and recruits from Bergamo are still the stuff of the theatre? Yes, these puppets in the hands of Strehler are eminently theatrical and it comes as a pleasant surprise.'[19]

La vedova scaltra had a mixed reception. Here was a more celebrated play which the critics felt obliged to take seriously and they differed in their views as to how far Strehler had risen to the challenge fundamental to Goldoni's theatrical reform: that of integrating commedia figures with familiar middle-class life. Massimo Dursi, after making some meaningful comments on the problems of Goldoni production, goes on to a critical view of Strehler's achievement here; 'We get the impression sometimes that it is a mistake to take Goldoni too seriously: don't get me wrong, I'm not suggesting we shouldn't respect him. It's just that we ought to trust him rather than revere him, listen to him, just as we listen to a familiar and friendly speaker and not as though he were an elderly uncle who is reading us his spiritual life-story. Strehler isn't the sort of person who generally is guilty of the latter fault . . . but in this production he treats the text with more reverence than it needs . . .

the characters move about the stage with extreme care, as though they were carrying precious glass statues . . . yes, there is plenty of stage movement, but it's all phoney, and not kept on the go by any real sense of imagination.'[20] Roberto Rebora, however, felt Strehler's aim was 'to remove those features which conventional interpretations have imposed on Goldoni in order to arrive at the true clarity and reality of the poetic work'. For Alberto Bertolini the show was too sophisticated in its staging and lacking in real speed. Strehler had not yet found the ideal piece to show off his own skills and – moreover – to alert his audience to the real, and hitherto unappreciated, strengths of Goldoni. That was to come a year later with his production of the *Villeggiatura* trilogy.

However, one event that contributed significantly to Strehler's growing appreciation and understanding of Goldoni had already taken place several years earlier. In 1948 – the second year of the Piccolo season – Strehler undertook a production of a work by Goldoni's great rival and enemy, Gozzi: *The Crow.* This is the only Gozzi play he has directed – he undertook another production with students of the Piccolo in 1954 – unless we count his two stagings of the Prokofiev opera *The Love of Three Oranges* at La Scala in 1947 and 1974. In 1970 Strehler prepared notes for a television film on the life of Goldoni which reveal his by now deep understanding of the man and the

6   The Arlecchino mask in action: Moretti in *L'amante militare,* 1951

playwright. He examines the problems Goldoni faced in his career and sees them as personal, artistic (his difficult attempt to instigate theatrical reform) and socio-political (his confrontation with Gozzi). This clash, Strehler argues, was truly destructive: a very different issue from the criticisms heaped on him earlier in his career by Chiari. Gozzi was a nobleman who recognised the challenge that Goldoni represented, and he was powerful enough (and clever enough as a writer) to destroy him. As Strehler puts it: Goldoni had to leave Venice; Gozzi stayed on. 'He remained, with his fables: part bet, part joke, part challenge – fun, yes, but nothing more. Goldoni was annihilated. One act of *Le baruffe* is enough to annihilate the whole of Gozzi; the lot: his nobility, his culture, everything else. When put face to face with *I rusteghi* Gozzi is a pygmy.'[21] It is important that Strehler should have directed one Gozzi work (it gives him more right to talk about the respective merits of the two rival Venetian dramatists) and not surprising that it should have been among the least successful of his productions. Interestingly enough, in the context of the versions of *Arlecchino*, this staging of *The Crow* – with additional gags, added dialogue, contemporary references – adapted the fable so as to present a company of actors rehearsing and performing the Gozzi piece in the square of a coastal village. The three 'heroic' characters in the play, Jennaro, Milla and Armilla, could scarcely be performed by the comic actors and therefore Strehler hit on the ingenious expedient of bringing three statues to life to take part. This did not save the show. As Silvio d'Amico pointed out: 'the splendid scenery and costumes, the charming music and dances didn't give the show – whose plot has always remained incomprehensible – a unity, a *raison d'être*, even a fundamentally technical one; the result was all too imprecise, too amateur, all too often descending to the level of a review or a circus; and it goes without saying that it was lacking in the true acrobatic skills of comedians of either the past or the present-day circus.'[22]

The production of the *Villeggiatura* trilogy in 1954 – coming midway between the second and third versions of *Arlecchino* – established Strehler as a master interpreter of Goldoni. The strength of the production lay in its portrayal both of a complex network of psychological relationships and of a society at a crucial point in history. What makes the play so modern, Strehler argues, is the sense of a whole age which is dying. He explains more fully: 'it is the story of *people* who live, suffer, amuse themselves, fall in love; but behind all this we are aware of the structure of a *society* on the threshold of the French revolution, moving towards that historical catastrophe with its own burden of humanity, of error, of the good, the bad and the incomprehensible'.[23]

Cesare Vico Lodovici drew attention to the originality of Strehler's approach: 'He has understood that the fault of the nineteenth century, even in the case of brilliant individual interpretations on the part of great actors of the past, was to look no further than the story itself; and that it is precisely by not stopping here, fascinating and alive though the story is, that we appreciate the full significance of this author who is much greater than he appears at first sight; and who only in this century, in recent years (we may add as of last night), is finally revealing what – beyond the lightness and musicality of the words – the real complexity and strength of his dramatic language is.'[24]

Strehler put a whole middle-class world on stage in the production with a directness and a depth of social awareness which both delighted and surprised the critics. Though – as Strehler points out – the plays had always enjoyed a high critical reputation, it was the first time they had been presented together. Only the first of the dramas, *The Anxieties*, has held the stage (it is the most immediately comic and is still frequently performed on its own). The other two, *The Adventures* and *The Return* – though clearly planned by Goldoni as part of an interrelated trio – were, until Strehler's production, neglected works. Neglected masterpieces, the critics were to discover, in their exploration of the heroine's dilemma, itself emblematic of the folly of a society destroying itself with an adherence to false values. The first play centres round Giacinta's tormenting behaviour to Leonardo and his conse-quent changes of heart and mind over the planned holiday which in turn affects his family, friends and servants. In the central drama she is forced to come to terms with the fact that her behaviour has led her into a marriage to a man she does not love; and in the final play this reality – as well as the intransigent and related problem of money – is faced, with all the consequences implicit for the different characters. Gastone Geron describes Strehler's skill in bringing out the interrelated levels of the play: 'The conclusion, which firmly establishes the social norm, is the price the dramatist must pay unless he chooses to ignore contemporary social mores; and Strehler has given powerful expression to the truth of a feeling which Goldoni never before and never afterwards allowed himself to be drawn to: an elegy for whatever dies silently, resigns gently, accepts the bad things in life: whilst portraying a society about to crumble tragically apart a century before we witness the disturbing tensions in Chekhov – to whose drama Strehler's *Villeggiatura* trilogy has been often compared.'[25]

Here was a production which triumphantly challenged the celebrated opinion held by the nineteenth-century literary critic de Sanctis, who claimed that 'Goldoni lacks that divine melancholy which is indispensable to the comic poet'. The elegiac quality was basic to Strehler's interpretation, as indeed it is to the original. He pointed out: 'What interests us is the effect of the show. We're interested in what this work says, and we are operating with the maximum amount of objectivity. We don't care for interpretative games with the classics'. Such 'interpretative games' were absent from a production which – even more forcefully in its subsequent Vienna and Paris stagings, designed by Ezio Frigerio – explored the issues of the play within the framework of a clear simple set. This was a far cry from the Goldoni of Eleonora Duse, who encouraged her company before a presentation of *La locandiera* with the memorable words: 'Goldoni must be performed with silk stockings, lace on the cuffs, with bows and lorgnettes ... a special eighteenth-century ... atmosphere ... true Goldoni ... we need spirited acting, fire, elegance in our voices and movement.'[26] These features played little or no part in the Strehler staging, which was the opposite of what the critic Renato Simoni had described (in 1932) as the accepted tradition of playing Goldoni: 'one in which languidness triumphs'. In certain respects Strehler's revolutionary approach resembles that of William Gaskill, who in his productions of the English post-Restoration drama in the 1960s banished a tradition of affected high comedy and elaborate staging with a Brechtian sparseness and emphasis on social and political realities.

We gain an important insight into Strehler's method if we examine the way in which he adapted the plays. The three individual dramas are complete in themselves and in order to reduce the trilogy to a one-evening entertainment Strehler cut them substantially. But his cuts go well beyond the technical; he achieved an alteration of emphasis, a shift of dramatic values which amounts to a significant modernisation of the plays. Strehler cut whole scenes that did not advance the action. More significantly, he adapted a crucial aspect of Goldoni's dramatic method, his technique of soliloquy and aside, in order to be rid of a convention which did not suit his idea of a more realistic interpretation of the works. Two examples will illustrate his method and achievement. In *The Return* Leonardo visits Giacinta (his future wife), who refuses to see him. He is aware of the reasons for her coolness, but his sexual jealousy is subordinate to his financial interest: if the marriage does not go forward he is ruined. Giacinta's maid tells him her mistress is indisposed and leaves. This gives rise to a lengthy soliloquy in which Leonardo expresses the full complexity of his feelings. In Strehler's version this was reduced to one line – 'Yes, it's no more than I deserve; I deserve worse' – the rest being expressed in terms of action. Here are the stage directions in Strehler's version:

Leonardo, left alone after Brigida has gone off, stands like a statue, he doesn't know whether to go or to stay. Then, suddenly, he makes a move towards the door on the right. He is about to go in and confront Giacinta. He stops in his tracks, his arms droop and he turns away in despair. He remains numb for a moment, letting the implications sink in.

Meanwhile the door at the back opens and Cecco (his servant) is seen, wearing an overcoat, carrying a wet umbrella.[27]

These stage directions translate a long soliloquy into physical theatrical movement. At another point, when Giacinta and Guglielmo (the man she really loves) meet – and part – for the last time Goldoni has Guglielmo say: 'Oh, God! I don't know whether I'm alive or not. She has confused me to such an extent that I don't know what to say!' whilst Giacinta has the following aside: 'Ah! no one would believe what an effort this is taking! It is costing me too much! It is giving me great pain!' As Lunari points out, the conversion of verbal soliloquy into stage action and the substitution of the above asides by a lengthy and powerful dramatic silence are what Strehler means when he says that he 'took into consideration the fact that Goldoni was being performed now, and therefore repetitions, statements that were too explicit, soliloquies and asides were cut'.[28] The implications of this were powerful; Lunari says that Goldoni suddenly seemed to have been writing at the end of the nineteenth, not the eighteenth, century. Why, he asks, did Goldoni himself not make these cuts and alterations in the play (written in 1761), the second last from his Venetian period? Because, he concludes, these soliloquies and asides were a convention which could be treated by Goldoni's, ideal, 'reformed' actor essentially as stage-directions, key references to states of mind and motivation, and yet permit the old fashioned actor to articulate verbally the crucial emotions of the character. Strehler excised what he felt to be an outmoded convention in favour of a gestic technique more appropriate to epic theatre. This is the main reason why critics felt that he had made Goldoni so contemporary. Without doing violence to the basic structure of the original, he had found a way of investing eighteenth-century dramatic method with a vital new life.

With his production of Le baruffe chiozzotte ten years later (1964) Strehler scored an even more remarkable success. The play – which also dates from Goldoni's final years in Venice – is a perfect complement to the Villeggiatura trilogy in that it marks the playwright's further rejection of the middle class in a celebration of a simple working community. Instead of a rich panorama of bourgeois life such as characterises the Villeggiatura, which shifts between a number of households in Livorno and the country, Le baruffe is set on a wooden jetty in Chioggia overlooked by a group of fishermen's houses, the one change of scene being to the courtroom where the Cogitore, Isidoro, sorts out the squabbles that are the subject of the drama. Here the trilogy's complex pattern of social and psychological relationships gives way to the dramatisation of a small community in which the tiniest (apparent) indiscretion can lead to a whole sequence of quarrels and recriminations. The harmless flirting of Lucietta and Toffolo gives rise to gossip which reaches the ear of Lucietta's fiancé, Titta Nane, who breaks off the engagement, thus encouraging another girl, Checca, who loves him, to hope she may become his wife.

Strehler's great skill was to present this eighteenth-century world of fishermen and their families in the small town of Chioggia with total conviction, thus destroying the received critical impression that the play was a colourful piece of folklore, far removed from psychological and social reality. The staging was anything but colourful. Here the influence of Brecht was very strongly felt in the bareness of the setting and the clothes, which were not those of conventional theatrical peasants (familiar from such works as *Giselle* or *Coppelia*), but heavy drab practical garments appropriate to the characters' way of life. The real power of the production lay in its convincing portrayal of people at work: from the fishermen, newly returned from a long trip at sea, through the seller of sliced pumpkin, to the women busy with their crochet frames. The opening scene with the women of the two households exchanging brief comments punctuated by the rattling of the frames on which they are painstakingly constructing the *merletti* was a tableau of striking social observation equalled by that of the arrival of the men with the boat, wrapped up as they are in thick woollen garments. The production gave a strong impression of the hardship of their lives, the loneliness brought

7   The arrival of the boat in *Le baruffe chiozzotte*

about by the long periods of separation. The staging was bathed in a clear but harsh wintery light, heavy and unromantic.

The establishing of a precise historical reality allowed the story to develop convincingly and rationally out of the context. Toffolo's gift of the slice of fried pumpkin to Lucietta, the gossiping it gives rise to, the partly malicious, partly innocent exploitation of this by Checca and her family all lead to the violent confrontation between Titta Nane and Lucietta, a scene of fiery emotional conviction in which the psychological conflict was locked into an awareness of the social mores which govern their actions, conditioning her frustrated rage and his jealous pride. To watch this scene (the production was filmed) is to be aware of Strehler's total commitment to the characters and situation, which are here treated with the same seriousness and care he gives to the acknowledged classics of the Shakespearian or Chekhovian repertoire. The vivid evocation of this world is matched and in part explained by Strehler's identification with the person of Isidoro. Goldoni himself was clearly creating in this character – the only one outside the world of the fishermen and their families by the virtue of his job and social status – a figure near to autobiography. In 1728 Goldoni had held precisely Isidoro's position of Cogitore, or legal adviser, at Chioggia. There is a parallel with Strehler here in that the director shares Goldoni's recognition of the nature of the middle-class artist's rapport with this community. His attitude is one of love and care, but he can never enter their society. Isidoro remains a lonely figure (this is particularly evident in his handling of the women he interviews); he reaches some sort of bond with Titta Nana, but the young man's working-class pride sets him in a world apart. As old Vincenzo, suspicious of Isidoro's interest in the women, comments: 'These gentlemen with their wigs don't go well with fishermen like us.' The director's realistic portrayal of Isidoro is a pointer to his own social and political stance.

If Strehler's production of Le baruffe was felt to be 'definitive' – and this epithet was employed by many critics – the staging of Il campiello in 1975 was considered even more of an achievement. Some of the features of the costumes and set (as with Le baruffe, the work of Luciano Damiani) carried the element of Brechtian realism a stage further, and there was an exploitation of the implications of the space on Strehler's part which revealed a deepening and extension of his powers of observation. The work is far more familiar in the Italian repertoire than Le baruffe, but it was Strehler's skill in this instance to reveal beyond the observation of everyday life (nothing remarkable happens in the play) a wealth of hitherto unexplored subtleties in the psychological and social relationships.

Strehler's exploration of Goldoni has been a process closely related to his work on Brecht. It is not only that the two writers have certain affinities in their dramatisation of working-class and bourgeois values, and that Strehler has gradually employed a more marked degree of starkness in the realism of his Goldoni stagings; there is also – as Strehler subtly argues – a more fascinating historical parallel in the development of the two playwrights. His analogy is worth quoting at length before we move on in a subsequent chapter to examine his productions of Brecht:

Goldoni's method, whereby the undisciplined masked characters were forced into a contradictory relationship with a precisely formulated written text, is the perfect equivalent of Brecht's move from the individualistic anarchy of expressionism to the epic (and narrative) rigour of the didactic pieces. In both cases we are dealing with a transitional stage in the playwright's development, of necessity limited in effect, or – shall we say – not yet capable of a full range of expression. When Goldoni takes the traditional features away from the masked figures and grounds them in a corresponding contemporary social reality (making Arlecchino a servant – with the characteristics of a specific social world – rather than some abstract concept of a servant, or making Pantalone not *the* merchant but *a* merchant complete with name and surname), so Brecht goes beyond the formal didactic technique of the *Lehrstück* to give the characters, and all the other theatrical features, that more complex dramatic structure which results both from the fusion of individual, personal and psychological features, and from the ability to discover precise connotations and references to wider historical and social realities.[29]

His notes on the production of *Il campiello* in 1975 draw particular attention to the precise social concerns basic to this drama, thrown into a powerful fresh light in his staging. Two issues were of major significance to Strehler. The first was the relationship between the working-class people who inhabit the campiello and the three outsiders – Gasparina, her uncle Fabrizio, and the Cavaliere (who all aspire to, or are descended from, loftier social backgrounds). The snobbery of Gasparina, the blunt lack of sympathy for the inhabitants of the square on the part of Fabrizio and the Cavaliere's complex relationship with the ordinary people were all realised with fresh subtlety and force. Most revealing was the presentation of the Cavaliere who is staying (during carnival) at the locanda in the square, who treats the local inhabitants to a generous feast, but who is inevitably marginalised and excluded. This Strehler emphasised in the introduction, immediately after the meal, of exuberant dances in which he does not take part and by having him remain alone in the square whilst the different characters drink his health, toasting to him through the window of the locanda. Strehler's presentation of the Cavaliere was, however, unsentimental: he sees – as Goldoni did – his generosity as a privilege of the wealthy.

The other feature of sharp social observation relates to the specific geography of the square and to Strehler's employment of the stage space. He observes that the social mores are clearly defined and rigorous. The houses which adjoin the square (there are four, as well as the locanda) are the private and personal domain of the four families. The windows and balconies act as natural areas of escape for the girls. None of the young people in the play has a father, the generation gap being strongly emphasised in the production. Strehler speaks of the 'virtually tribal rituals' of this society. The girls, for instance, are permitted on the balconies and can talk to other friends, including the boys who are allowed to move freely about the square. This privilege is denied the young women, who can only come into the square and socialise when accompanied by their mothers. At one point one of the girls, Gnese, wants to give an artificial flower she has made to her friend Lucietta, who lives on the other side of the square. She speaks to a boy in the square named Zorzetto and asks him to give the flower to Lucietta. He suggests she throw it to him, but she doesn't want to damage it, so she lowers the flower to him in a basket and he takes it across to Lucietta. In Strehler's production the scene emerged with added poignancy through its powerful combination of social and psychological observation, the flower being in its turn a subtle love token from Gnese to Zorzetto.

Damiani's set was conspicuously different from that for *Le baruffe*. This one was much simpler, the four houses being two-dimensional and any sense of perspective illusion being avoided. But the set projected well into the auditorium, thus involving the audience, though not in any conventional naturalistic way. The fourth wall, in short, was dispensed with and the space given an added dynamism. This was reinforced by a novel addition: the ground was covered with snow (made from polystyrene). This gave the space a more tactile quality, the snow being more than a mere scenic decoration. As Massimo Gallerani points out: 'The snow lies on the ground, piled in heaps near the walls; a light insubstantial element mixed with the streamers from the carnival. It provides a game for Zorzetto, who happily slides on it, an extra labour for Pasqua and her broom, a curious novelty for the Cavaliere, a weapon for Zorzetto in his fight with Catte, but above all a diversion for everyone. For people who have fun with very little, who look on amazed at a small natural phenomenon and make the most of it, turning a potential nuisance into a game; but it's done lightly, not overstated: a slide here . . . a few snowballs thrown there . . .'[30] We can leave the final word on this show – and on Strehler's Goldoni stagings – with Gallerani (who worked on the production, documenting it), as he sums up the basic subject of Strehler's interest, underlining the total integration of his dramatic concerns and their theatrical representation:

In Strehler and Damiani's staging the sky, the walls, the windows, the balconies, the steps, the snow, the streamers, the puddles are not the mere external setting, the more or less abstract framework in which to place the goings on of a little square; they *are* the square as much as the characters are; just like the characters they speak, react, become helpers or opponents . . . in a word they are always deeply bound up with what is happening, with the characters; they are a constant point of reference, something alive, substantial: they narrate the story of a community which wouldn't be what it is without this specific sky and these particular walls and windows.[31]

8   Damiani's set, covered in snow and extending well into the auditorium, for *Il campiello*, 1975

4   Power games: Strehler and Shakespeare

I'm certain of one thing: that I have to approach Shakespeare with great caution and care. Get under the surface of the text, but never go against it or abuse it. That – it seems to me – is the only viable way. He is a very demanding, tyrannical author; he requires total commitment. Shakespeare is that mountain range which separates those who play with theatre from those who believe in it.

Strehler in Ugo Ronfani, *Io, Strehler: Conversazioni con Ugo Ronfani*, p. 137

The pattern of Strehler's work on Shakespeare is very different from that which characterises his stagings of either Brecht or Goldoni. With Brecht he began relatively late in his career and all his Brecht stagings have been of major significance. In the case of Goldoni he has gradually matured in a manner which to a marked degree mirrors the playwright's own artistic development. The 1947–8 season saw him undertaking two Shakespeare productions, one of *The Tempest*, Shakespeare's late (some would argue last) play; during the five-year period 1948–52 he staged seven Shakespeare dramas, of all types: history, tragedy, comedy. Gradually after this the rate of the Shakespeare stagings slowed down: only two were undertaken between 1952 and 1957; no more until 1964; then a long break (interrupted by a revival) until 1972; and a further gap (again interrupted by a revival – of the same piece) before his last production to date, in 1978. Looking back over this sequence of productions a significant pattern emerges: the last two – *The Tempest* (1978) and *King Lear* (1972) – rank amongst the finest of all his work: they are equal to productions of Shakespeare anywhere in the world. The two preceding shows – *Il gioco dei potenti* (*Power Games*) (an adaptation of the first historical trilogy first staged in 1964 and revived twice, in 1973 and 1975 in Salzburg and Berlin respectively) and *Coriolanus* (1957) – marked a maturity of style resulting from two significant factors: his encounter with Brecht and his decision to mount far fewer productions. The 1955–6 season was the determining one in each case; he undertook only three productions at the Piccolo, the second of which was *The Threepenny Opera*, his first – and highly acclaimed – staging of Brecht.

Coriolanus marks a watershed. From then on his Shakespeare stagings were to be prepared with far more care and attention; more significantly he had found in the ethics and staging devices of epic theatre a *raison d'être* for his productions. They ceased to be essays in style, praiseworthy for their variety and versatility: the plays Strehler undertook from then on were the right ones: the one he *had* to direct. Another factor to be borne in mind

63

alongside the influence exerted by Brecht is the importance of three opera productions undertaken in the decade 1971–80. For the first time Strehler turned to operatic adaptations of Shakespeare, with *Macbeth* (1975) and *Falstaff* (1980). (He had previously directed both Shakespeare's *Macbeth* and – though never *The Merry Wives* – *Henry IV Part I*.) This pair becomes a trio of Verdi stagings – which received the highest critical praise for their originality and total integration of dramatic and musical values – if we include *Simon Boccanegra* (1971), arguably Strehler's finest operatic staging to date. All three were performed at La Scala, Milan; indeed they opened the season there on 7 December, the feast of St Ambrose (patron saint of Milan), the most prestigious date in the Italian theatrical calendar. Though *Boccanegra* is not directly a Shakespearian opera, it is – as will be argued later – paradoxically the most Shakespearian of all in structure and mood. The increasing complexity in the dialectic of Strehler's Shakespeare stagings is attributable to the fact that he operates between two opposed poles: epic theatre and grand opera.

It is important to examine the work from *Coriolanus* onwards with increasing attention to the reasons for staging and the details of performance. The productions undertaken in the first decade at the Piccolo do not merit this level of research, though it is crucial to observe at this point the features which link the works and map out what – at this point in time – appears a course governed by that intuitive compass which was guiding Strehler and the company. The first Shakespeare play chosen was *Richard II*, in 1948, the same year Strehler first staged *The Tempest* (in Florence in the open air – though with the Piccolo company). These now seem significant choices: the wheel comes full circle with the second production of *The Tempest* thirty years later; whilst the choice of a history play points forward to the productions of the three parts of *Henry VI (Il gioco dei potenti)*, which Strehler has reworked twice, on each occasion with a different company and in radically different stagings. It is not insignificant that the history plays take up a large part of the Strehler canon: they are in no way the dramas most frequently performed in Italy, and for a major cultural reason. Italian theatre has been dominated by the figure of the *mattatore*, the actor-director who dominates the show. Italy's theatrical traditions have not in the long run been seriously affected by the movement in Europe towards the formation of permanent companies and the rise of the director – Strehler and the Piccolo remain the exception. The earliest Shakespeare productions at the Piccolo should be seen in this light: as directorial pieces showing off the company ensemble, rather than as vehicles for bravura performance.

This explains the choice of *Richard III* in 1950. Memories of Olivier's Shakespeare films were still strong (in the critics minds as well as in Strehler's) but there was no attempt to perform this play as a star vehicle. The critics spoke instead of the relentless tread of the production, which had a single setting serving for the exterior as well as the interior scenes, suffused with heavy darkness – thus giving the impression of a 'funeral rite, celebrated under the emblem of death'.[1]

The production of *Henry IV Part I* in the following year (1951) had stronger echoes of Olivier's stagings. It was mounted out of doors in the Roman Theatre at Verona, where a vast reconstruction of an Elizabethan theatre was undertaken. Critics compared both this production and the earlier *Richard II*, which had also been staged simply, following Elizabethan canons, to Olivier's *Henry V*. Clearly the challenge in these productions lay in

9   The Elizabethan stage built inside the Roman Theatre at Verona for Shakespeare's *Henry IV*, 1951

exploring different theatrical conventions. In *Henry IV* Strehler introduced *sbandieratori* (flag-wavers characteristic of the Palio at Siena), a large vocal chorus and a series of brilliant encounters between armed soldiers which were to anticipate his techniques when mounting the Wars of the Roses trilogy much later. Falstaff was played by Camillo Pilotto, but reviewers sang his praises less than they did those of his band of ill-assorted recruits (taken from Part II): a feature illustrative of Strehler's political concerns, which were to find full expression in the episode with Jack Cade in the first tetralogy and the scene of the rebellious citizens which opens *Coriolanus*.

The production of *The Taming of The Shrew* was another even clearer example of a play chosen to show off the strengths of the company. This was a version of the play in which – according to Angelo Spadavecchia – 'the significance of Petruchio and that of Katherina was diminished, and in which the ensemble became the main character: the comic clowning of the drunken Christopher Sly [Strehler characteristically expanded Shakespeare's skeletal play-within-the-play structure, having Sly persistently intervene in the main action from his room over the stage], the caricatures of the gentlemen from Padua, the commedia servants. A wonderful show, loud, constantly on the move, inspired, frenetic.' He concludes: 'a further demonstration of the fact that Strehler is the only Italian director who can bring the commedia dell'arte to life for us'.[2] The staging of *Twelfth Night* (1951) met with very little success; Strehler had not found a native theatrical style to match the very different pace of this play. His *Macbeth* in the following year is significant in pointing forward to the staging of the Verdi opera two decades later. Already we find critics complaining of Strehler's addiction to underlighting. Simoni wrote an essentially favourable review in which he praises the original expedient of dividing the stage vertically into two levels so as to throw some of the key events – the appearance of the witches ('like great birds flapping their wings, and bathed in a sickly green light') or the sleepwalking scene – into sharper relief, but ends by commenting wryly: 'But I would have liked to see a bit more of the action.'[3] The *Julius Caesar* production (1954) – which may now seem like a preparation for the far more significant *Coriolanus* three years later – was another interesting choice for Strehler: of a work as much political play as personal tragedy, in which there is no single dramatic protagonist. The setting was one of the most outstanding and original features; it was created by Piero Zuffi and consisted of a fixed structure resembling an amphitheatre in front of which a smaller semi-circle of columned doors and windows could be superimposed to facilitate the contrast between the incidents leading up the main action (with the conspirators, for instance, meeting in darkened niches) and the key events taking part on the main stage. It is significant that in this period Strehler had not found a permanent scenic designer with whom he could collaborate fruitfully on equal terms. The production of *Coriolanus*, on the other hand, was designed by Ezio Frigerio and the costumes were the work of Luciano Damiani: the two artists who were to work with Strehler throughout the rest of his theatrical career.

Before discussing this key production it is useful to glance at the one play in this first phase of Shakespearian research which was to be taken up by Strehler later: the open-air *Tempest* of 1948. Though very different from the production first seen at the Teatro Lirico thirty years later, the staging at the Boboli gardens in Florence revealed some of the features which were to manifest themselves more fully in the second version. Strehler utilised for his setting the lake known as the Vasca dei Cigni (the swans' pool), which has at its centre a fountain representing Neptune. It was necessary to build Prospero's island, a construction of gigantic proportions recalling the work of Reinhardt, in the centre of the lake. The various locations on the island – Prospero's cell, Caliban's grotto and so forth – were placed in a landscape inspired partly by medieval theatre and partly by renaissance chivalric poetry. The implications of medieval pageant staging were present not only in the employment of individual locations for separate scenes but in the symbolic significance of the fact that the basest actions and the lowest forms of civilisation were restricted to the outer edges of the setting whilst the movement towards redemption and experience – on the part of Ferdinand, for instance – was signified by the gradual ascent to the higher area towards the centre of the island. It is particularly interesting to note that the roles of Trinculo and Stephano were interpreted as commedia figures: Pulcinella and Brighella respectively – a feature which was to be considerably expanded in the later version. In this earlier staging Strehler made the most of the scenic and musical features of the celebratory masque (a device omitted in the second staging), having the parts of the goddesses played by opera singers. The music – arrangements of Scarlatti by Fiorenzo Carpi – introduced at this point a baroque reference which Ettore Gaipa (who played the Boatswain in the production) argues 'underlined the rediscovery of human values, the journey to a new world, a voyage into the future'.[4]

Strehler was well aware when undertaking his production of *Coriolanus* in 1957 that here was one of Shakespeare's final and most complex dramas. He comments, however, on the lack of useful criticism (he found Hazlitt most helpful) and the rare occasions on which the work had been performed. Peter Hall's celebrated production at Stratford with Olivier, which occasioned a major revaluation of the play in Britain, was two years away; Strehler's achievement in staging the work is therefore all the more remarkable. He asks what sort of play *Coriolanus* is – tragedy or historical drama – thus anticipating the major issues of dramatic criticism in the early sixties, and his conclusion is significant:

We have defined *Coriolanus* as a 'historical tragedy', or better still, a 'political' tragedy, understanding by the term 'political' the full range of references implied: political in the sense of the dialectical progress of history; historical in the sense of the complex relationship between different groups and their contrast of interests; and within these groups, within these different social classes, the clash of interests between the individual, his own class and the opposing one; and finally the struggle within the individual himself in conflict with his innate contradictions.[5]

Strehler refused to restrict the meaning of the work by presenting either the story of a tragic hero narrated within a political context, or the story of a society in which the fate of the individual is relatively unimportant. His method – whether in analysing the play or in staging it – was, he argues, neither 'romantic' nor 'idealistic', but 'dialectical'. In this way the contradictions of the play were not solved in any neat way but exposed in all their complexity. It is significant that Strehler had had his first, overwhelming encounter with Brecht two years previously – both with the man and his work; and that he was preparing a production of *The Good Person of Setzuan* whilst engaged on *Coriolanus*. This Shakespeare staging tells us a great deal about his approach to Brecht and the implications of epic theatre. His aim is not to diminish the emotional and theatrical appeal of the work by emphasising a particular political viewpoint. Rather, the approach is consistently concerned to explore the rich pattern of paradoxes within the play. With his production of *Lear* later Strehler said that he wanted to make the drama appear simultaneously immensely complex and crystal clear; he first achieved this miracle of Shakespearian staging with *Coriolanus*.

For Strehler the conflicts between the social and political classes in Rome (the plebeians and the patricians) open out into conflicts within the separate groups to lead finally to a conflict between nations: between the Romans and the Volscians. Coriolanus is at the centre of all these conflicts and his position is both ambiguous and dangerous. It is Tullus Aufidius who for Strehler expresses most clearly the key to the tragedy in his lines:

> So our virtues
> Lie in the interpretation of the time,
> And power, unto itself most commendable,
> Hath not a tomb so evident as a chair
> T'extol what it hath done.
> One fire drives out one fire; one nail one nail;
> Rights by rights falter; strengths by strengths do fail.

– 'a comment', he points out, 'which could not more perfectly express the dialectical concept of history and the rejection of the abuse of force as a permanent type of injustice'.[6]

Strehler chose to direct the play in an epic style, with a very simple staging (by Frigerio) and historically accurate costumes (by Damiani). In terms of acting this called for essentially two things: a constant awareness of the ambiguities of situation, and a performance style which meant acting in the third person, maintaining an objective distance from the role rather than being immersed in the character in a naturalistic Stanislavskian way. An example from the beginning of the play will illustrate Strehler's refusal to allow the actors to take sides simplistically. He mentions elsewhere in an essay on Brecht that he had seen the German dramatist with a copy of *Coriolanus* (the play fascinated Brecht, who was still engaged on an adaptation when he died) and this had made him burst out: 'Why do you want to do Coriolanus? It's horrible, fascist, impossible. Coriolanus is a ghastly figure, bursting with pride', to which Brecht had replied: 'Now then, young man, give it a bit more thought, review the issue. Perhaps it's not entirely as you think, perhaps it can be seen from another point of view',[7] and had gone on to tell Strehler to look more closely at the characters of the tribunes Sicinius and Junius. He did, and found that they were far more complex than he had first considered. This led him eventually to a more subtle presentation of the people they represent – the plebeians, notably in the opening scene. Strehler insisted they should not be seen as a clumsy and unruly crowd, easily ridiculed. They present a real threat and therefore must be armed. This in no way detracts from their awkwardness and boorishness but it shows another side of the issue, opening up the dialectic in respect of the class conflict. For this reason Strehler is highly critical of Weckwerth, who directed Brecht's adaptation of *Coriolanus* after the playwright's death and who avoided any ambiguity in the play's opening scene, making the crowd too crudely comic. He comments: 'It is obvious: if you take away the positive attributes of the crowd (weapons, force, decisiveness) you mustn't overdo the negative attributes. It is true that in this way you do reach a certain balance in the negative versus positive aspects of the crowd, but via a levelling down, rather than by confronting the text as it stands brim full of dialectical contradictions.'[8] One glimpses in such a difference of views why Strehler is Brecht's true heir.

Strehler's solution to the conflict of tragedy and history, of the individual versus society, was to divide the staging into two clearly separate halves:

The two acts represent two different ways of looking at the same reality but in different registers: the collective and the personal. Act I shows the leading characters of the tragedy in a historical context, predominantly a political one – but aren't politics and history made by individuals? Act II defines the leading characters in a psychological, personal, human context – but aren't the workings of history human? isn't the individual an inescapable part of the group?[9]

This is the Brechtian *Verfremdungseffekt* in action. The structure thus
established allowed the great scene of confrontation between Coriolanus and
Volumnia to have its full emotional value as a classically Aristotelian
example of reversal (peripeteia) and recognition (anagnorisis) which culmi-
nates in Coriolanus's realisation of his error in the line: 'Oh mother mother,
what have you done?', yet at the same time to do something more than effect
a straightforward catharsis. Strehler drives straight to the heart of the matter
in analysing the scene, pointing out that the monster has become human but
it is too late for him to undergo a permanent change: 'Coriolanus can no
longer be what he has been up to now, but neither is he capable of becoming
something new.' There is here a combination of human and political insight
characteristic of the mature Strehler. 'One had assumed', comments Giorgio
Prosperi, 'that Strehler would have directed Carraro to perform in a style
which distanced the character completely. It didn't work like that. Once the
bloodthirsty hero had come off his pedestal, though his eyes still retained
some satanic flashes, he was seen in a powerfully new light: in a human
context, so that in the famous scene with his mother he struck a note of
intense and manly emotion.'[10] Cesare Vico Lodovici writes that in this scene
'Strehler revealed his skill in gauging the power of pauses and of silence in the
theatre: more effective than any words or movement.'[11] The stage direction

10   The confrontation scene in *Coriolanus*, 1957

at this point, 'Holds her by the hand, silent' – thought to be authorial – was realised with the maximum theatrical force.

The scenery by Damiani was designed to frame the action simply and emphasise the symmetrical structure of the drama, whose sharp dialectical confrontations were crystallised in the blocking. The setting was sparse: a plain white backcloth, a wooden floor (divided horizontally into three differently raised levels), and two high walls at right angles to this serving as wings with one large entrance each. No curves broke up this vertical and horizontal symmetry, which was further extended by the rigorous employment of a few architectural features repeated throughout the twenty-two scenes (or tableaux) into which the play was divided. Thus Marcius's house had a low wall upstage with a seat built into it; it was broken by two simple openings and decorated with a sundial. The only other feature was a thin tree stage right. The same essential structure was employed for Aufidius's home, varied with the addition of two columns and a different seat, the sundial replaced by a mural of two lions.

A series of arches and tents, confined to the upstage area, was utilised in other scenes. The opening scene had a simple sequence of five arches; for the senate scene two double arches with two solid benches at the sides and three separate seats, two under and one between the arches, defined the space in which the power game was played. A single arch was employed in several other scenes, most tellingly as a focal point in the final tableau, which showed two soldiers dragging Marcius's body across towards the stage right exit while Aufidius stood with two other soldiers by the opposite exit. The logic of this counterpoint and symmetry in the setting reached its height in the dramatic climax of the play: the confrontation of Coriolanus with his family. Three two-dimensional tents (descending in height towards stage left) had been employed to represent the rival army camps. In the Volumnia–Coriolanus scene the largest of these stood upstage centre with Marcius just downstage of it on the second level of the floor. To his right (on the same level) stood the three women (one holding his son close to her); to his left (still on this level) the other protagonist, Aufidius, flanked by two soldiers (on the highest level). Here the blocking, setting and costumes (the three women in black, the three Volscians in armour) neatly focused the inevitability of the position into which Coriolanus has been driven through his conflict of personal and political feelings.

It was eight years before Strehler returned to Shakespeare. With his two-part adaptation of the first historical trilogy (the three parts of *Henry VI*) as *Il gioco dei potenti* (*Power Games*) he took up and expanded the political issues central to his staging of *Coriolanus*. The influence of Brecht was, if anything, even stronger here, but its theatrical expression was very different. This was no austere production analysing (as in the case of *Coriolanus* or *Galileo*) the paradoxes implicit in a mature work; here was an entertainment (closer to *The Threepenny Opera*) which explored the dramatic variety of a play written at the beginning of Shakespeare's career. It soon became known as Strehler's 'Shakespearian blockbuster', rich in its theatrical ingredients, guaranteed to thrill the public: 'feasts, fairs, battles, rebellions, throne-rooms, executions, love, hate, vengeance, deception, apparitions, skulls, grave-diggers, cannon shots'.[12] The critics referred not only to Brecht but to Strehler's other stagings including *El nost Milan*, claiming that the production was something akin to Fellini's *8½* as a summing-up of the director's previous work.

The reference to the Bertolazzi play draws attention to Strehler's concern here with the people, the crowd, the poor, who are – to quote the critic of *Il giorno* – 'by turn victims, puppets, or unconscious protagonists in the unfolding of their own history'. The central image of the play – concentrated in three contrasted battle scenes – was of a roundabout, a wild carousel of the struggle for power, which culminated in the final image of what Strehler describes as the 'dance of the youthful aspirants to the throne': a tableau of powerful gestic force with Richard of Gloucester spotlit, fists clenched, as richly-dressed couples whirl past. Strehler's Brechtian emphasis – on theatricality and a sequence of striking visual images – is very different from that of Hall and Barton in their Stratford staging of the plays two years previously where starkness of presentation accompanied a series of powerful individual performances. Strehler's vision of the central meaning of the trilogy is also different. He does not see the unfolding of the bloody story as a comment on the absurdity and futility of the power struggle; his approach is more positive:

It is definitely more convenient, more fashionable to claim that mankind is surrounded by torment, nothingness; but in my opinion it is more modern to have faith in mankind and his future. That is why *Il gioco* came into being as a modern production, a contemporary show, a challenge . . . [a show which] expresses a faith in the spoken word, in theatre as a human undertaking – one which is tentatively held together by the concrete reality of objects on stage, but which functions as a sounding board, a point of precise reference – faith too in the theatrical convention itself and in the imagination, faith in theatre as something which speaks to lots of people, entertaining but not hypnotising them, faith in the message which comes through by the end of every performance, faith in poetry, faith in history and those truths which poetry enshrines.[13]

Eight years later (1973) Strehler returned to the plays in a new staging for Salzburg. His notebooks express a particular concern about the need to revive the work. The production was a marked advance on the previous one, developing many of the ideas and images so as to give them added theatrical force. The first production had been conceived as a sort of dream or nightmare, a feature which dictated the pace of the action. In the Salzburg version the images of a roundabout and a circus combined to establish the mood and tempo. Strehler's initial image was of an octagonal shape covered up like a roundabout when the fair has closed. Inside this were three separate stages resembling circus rings on which various scenes took place simultaneously. 'The show must have the feel of something temporary: a bit like a cheap circus, with the ridiculous figure of a king, and powerful frightening figures who are a cross between savage animals and clowns – jaguars or poisonous oriental fish.'[14]

An example of the employment of simultaneous stage action – which also gives a clear idea of the nature of the adaptation – is the opening sequence. On the central stage the funeral of Henry V can be seen; to the left (in an area defined by a tree) children are singing and dancing whilst to the right we see the investiture of the boy king: Henry VI. In this tableau several children are being costumed so that in the end 'they turn into little monsters, little dwarves dressed as grown-ups'. As the central ceremony comes to an end the mourners in black go off to fetch the boy king. As they do so the costumes and the music change: from funeral to festive as the king is crowned. Meanwhile on the left the march of history reveals a mature Henry at his wedding: the figures of power visibly age. To celebrate the wedding a story-teller, assisted by a troupe of seven actors, narrates the fortunes of Joan of Arc. This incident considerably expanded a feature of Strehler's 1965 staging of the plays in which three *guitti* – coarse strolling players – acted the story of another supposed witch, Marjorie Jourdain.

The worlds of Brecht and Pirandello meet here and the influence of both playwrights can also be seen in the manner in which the two central props – the throne and the crown – were realised. The former was seen as 'a stool, old, mildewed with age and discoloured, which has served every possible function: in the kitchen as well as the stable. It is covered with a piece of gold cloth which has decoration made of paper and glass and is placed on a wooden plank so as to become a processional chair. The king is carried around in it like a pope who more clearly resembles a clown.' The crown was placed in a black case: it was made of tin, with cheap glass jewels, and was lopsided. Strehler comments: 'there is a life-and-death struggle for a case containing a relic made of tin and glass'. The ironic visual imagery of Brecht's *Edward II* mingles with the theatrical trappings of Pirandello's *Henry IV*.

The staging of the battles was particularly striking in its operatic bravura. As in the previous version Strehler distinguished clearly between the three major battle scenes, increasing the savagery of the weaponry on each successive encounter. He distinguished between the 'butchers' with their large leather aprons, their rubber boots and their equally modern helmets, and the 'soloists of death': the powerful figures in ritual armour, like samurai, masked and wearing frightening headgear. He saw the ordinary soldiers as interchangeable. As they are killed they are dragged offstage and thrown into heaps, but they bounce back again, clean themselves up, swap the red rose for the white, wipe the blood off their faces and go into battle again. 'The image is one of bloodstained puppets which fall down and get up again as soon as the strings are jerked.' In the Vienna staging (1975) this ritual acquired a new level of intensity, as Roberto De Monticelli points out: 'The show is a patterning of cruel symmetries. Every time the figures of power go into battle, divided between the factions of York and Lancaster, dressed impeccably in black leather, waving their slim maces like whips, the sound of something half-way between military and circus music sets the invisible wheel (or ladder) of their game in motion: a game to the death, for the possession of a throne, but a theatrical game as well, a bitter festivity, the poetic representation of a long history of slaughter.'[15] The paraphernalia of battle alternated with a different ritual: that of the gradual paring down of the action to basics, the movement towards an examination of human values glimpsed through suffering. The scene of the father who has killed his son and the son who has killed his father – one of the most poignant inheritances from the medieval morality – was given a central focus in the production and accompanied by very different music: the sound of a solo violin. If this scene powerfully evoked memories of *Lear* – the Strehler production which intervened between the first two versions of *Il gioco* – its staging also owed much to Strehler's love of lyric opera. Whilst preparing the Vienna staging of *Il gioco* he was busy preparing his monumental production of Verdi's *Macbeth* for La Scala.

The gap in time and achievement between Strehler's production of the Shakespearian original (in 1952) and his staging of Verdi's *Macbeth* was a large one. Shakespearian purists may recoil in horror from the Verdi, the work which was the crowning achievement of his early period, but for Strehler a knowledge of the play in no way diminishes his admiration for the opera. Indeed, he was to argue – and to demonstrate – that Verdi's genius extends the psychological implications of the situation in which the two protagonists find themselves, whilst his own analysis pushed these issues into a modern context. Verdi's insight, he claims, was to observe and probe more deeply into the isolation of the two central characters; they attempt, through crime, to forge some contact, but they merely succeed in making the abyss that separates them even deeper. Thus the tragedy of the ambitious wife and the vacillating husband 'becomes in Verdi's opera the drama of two lonely people who never meet, who drown in the void: Lady Macbeth in the madness of infantile regression; Macbeth in progressive self-destruction'. It is a very plausible thesis extended further in Strehler's Freudian approach to the staging. 'The witches and the apparitions in the cave', he goes on, 'straightforward concrete manifestations to Verdi and his contemporaries, must for us, in the modern world, be filtered through our awareness of Freud and of psychoanalysis. Macbeth's journey into the world of visions is a dark voyage to the centre of his own conscience: the only way we in the twentieth century can envisage a supernatural relationship. In reality these phantoms don't exist.'[16]

In the production – as in that of the Shakespeare – Strehler did not have Banquo's ghost appear on stage (and on both occasions many critics were disappointed). But there was nothing low-key about Macbeth's reaction in the opera as he threw himself on the hallucinatory figure, causing a cushion to explode and shower the stage with feathers as he fell to his knees sobbing. Verdi's *Macbeth* is grand opera and large-scale acting conventions are required to do it justice. Naturalism is not enough in opera (in any theatrical work, Strehler would argue); detailed psychological study and observation are necessary but the physical gesture has to function in a register which matches the music. It is possible to stage the Shakespeare by playing down very considerably the supernatural effects (William Gaskill and Adrian Noble have notably illustrated the effectiveness of this method); but it contradicts the score in the opera. Hence the scenes with the witches in Strehler's production took place under a huge veil floating over the whole stage onto which giant faces were projected for the apparitions. Strehler himself described it as representing a vast placenta; it gave visual form to Macbeth's subconscious, constantly changing shape and colour. The redness of this veil in the final act contrasted with the metallic glare of the copper backdrop, a texture taken up in the costumes of the soldiers, their shields and flags, as well as the branches of Birnam wood. The two protagonists were isolated in this implacable setting, whose harshness and sense of brooding menace were carried further in the appearance of a series of movable ramps which projected forward from the back of the stage to accommodate Duncan's retinue, Banquo's murderers, Birnam wood and the banquet scene. The last named had a sense of mystery and threat, reminding the music critic Teodoro Celli of a sinister tribunal about to pass sentence of death.

The vocal performances were highly praised: the recording testifies to the total integration of musical and dramatic effect. The conductor was Claudio Abbado, a vital collaborator who, with the designer, Damiani, has consistently revealed an insight and imagination to match that of Strehler. Abbado's approach was violent in the extreme, emphasising the savagery of the score. Verdi himself called for dramatic talents rather than beautiful voices in this work, notably in the role of Lady Macbeth. The sleepwalking scene in particular employs vocal and dramatic effects which point the way to the music theatre of the twentieth century. Shirley Verrett performed the scene making her way along a narrow wall, translating her own precarious psychological state into physical terms. The comments of Strehler on the score are significant, revealing that depth of musical knowledge and imagination which is the particular hallmark of his theatrical work:

Verdi's appreciation of Shakespeare is a romantic one. But within the limits this imposes he managed through his remarkable dramatic instinct and his critical and poetic sensibility to evolve a new approach which is both original and profound. The continual flashes of poetic insight are part of this talent: the first appearance in any score of detailed dramatic directions to the singer: 'speak in a whisper', 'the scene must be performed as quietly as possible with a hollow dark tone of voice', 'as quiet as possible, the voice wavering' – these anticipate the devices of modern theatre by a whole century. This musical and dramatic definition of the vocal texture is to all intents and purposes a directorial concept which illuminates the relationship of Macbeth and Lady Macbeth and goes straight to the heart of the psychological confusion of the two characters. This is how he was able to give expression to Shakespeare's ideas and to his own.[17]

If the emphasis in his *Macbeth* was an essentially psychological one, it was the political themes of *Simon Boccanegra* which were most fully brought out. Coming as it does in 1971, between the first two versions of *Il gioco* and a year before *Lear* this Verdi production was even more closely linked to the issues which were absorbing Strehler in his work on Shakespeare. The opera can with some truth be seen as even more Shakespearian in mood and theme than *Otello*, *Macbeth* and *Falstaff*. Indeed it has particular affinities with *Lear*, as Paolo Isotta has pointed out:

From *I vespri siciliani* onwards we find scattered in every opera shards and fragments of that work he lavished so much affection on and which he never completed: *King Lear*. If the Fifth Gospel is hidden, yet present somehow in the hearts of all men ('Search and you will find it in yourself'), Verdi's *King Lear* by the same token does exist: all we have to do is search for it patiently and reconstruct it limb by limb from some forty years of music. The work which contains more of this *Lear* than any other is *Simon Boccanegra*.[18]

This is not as fanciful as it may at first appear; Isotta's review appeared in 1976 when *Boccanegra* was revived at La Scala and his comments were inspired by Strehler's production.

There are strong echoes of *Lear*: the two principal characters are old men who have both lost a child (as they believe) and who experience a painful pilgrimage towards understanding. The hero dies after rediscovering his lost daughter and there is a scene of reconciliation with his enemy in the final act, which Fedele d'Amico has described as a 'Shakespearian duet'. The Shakespearian features go further than parallels with *Lear*. There is a conflict of political interests which has strong affinities with the history plays, a struggle which comes to a head in the great council scene where the plebeians break in and confront the patricians: an encounter which might have come from

Coriolanus. All these Shakespearian features undoubtedly fascinated Strehler in his choice of this work, though it was the political significance which most interested him:

The historical Simon who established a truly popular government attempts in the opera to bring about peace between the two most fundamentally opposed social groups, which may seem like a cosy compromise to us, but it wouldn't have appeared like that to Verdi's contemporaries, as the composer is repeating that cry for unification characteristic of the Risorgimento: 'The Adriatic coast and Liguria have a common fatherland.' The civic theme of the work is the one I have been able to explore in the greatest depth. I've had to keep the romantic story within the bounds of what is incredible historically but credible musically.[19]

Strehler brought to the production a wealth of political and social insight which completely overthrew the accepted view of the work as a minor unsuccessful piece. It is interesting that Verdi completely reworked the opera (first performed in 1857) in 1881, when he had returned to composition after a long break and begun his collaboration with Boito, who wrote the librettos for *Otello* and *Falstaff*. Strehler himself must have appreciated and sympathised with this process of revision. The production's most striking innovation was the prologue, concerned – like Prospero's narration to Miranda – with events in the 'dark backward and abysm of time'. Because the audience is bombarded with a quick succession of characters who will reappear in the main action, which takes place twenty-five years later, it has been considered a very clumsy piece of exposition on the part of Verdi and his librettist, Piave. Strehler solved this by presenting the sequences of confrontations as isolated events taking place in a dream, glimpsed in a flashback. Out of the pitch dark different characters loomed briefly, separated from one another in the vast space. The dreamlike element was emphasised in the way Simon knocked on the door of Fiesco's palace: he raised his fists and pounded the air in slow motion; it turned into nightmare when he discovered the dead body of Maria. Instead of merely going offstage he emerged from the shadows – we had been taken inside the palace – and the scene was mimed in front of us. Strehler kept his *coup de théâtre* until the very end of the act when, in sharp contrast to the pervading gloom, the stage flooded with light whilst a vast crowd arrived to hoist Simon on their shoulders and celebrate his election as doge. The brash music here – often dismissed as reminiscent of a brass band – took on new meaning as a savage ironic emphasis of the gap between the public celebration and the private grief of the protagonist.

Lear – the work *par excellence* which dramatises the conflict between public power and private suffering – opened, in Strehler's production (1972), with a scene of formal ceremony, once again set in a far-off world, dreamy and mysterious. The 'love test' that initiates the action took place behind a transparent veil drawn across the stage like a Brechtian traverse curtain. The veil also represented the map of the kingdom Lear intends to divide. The stage was bathed in half-light, the figures static and majestically dressed. This was Strehler's solution to one of the problems that had vexed him from the start: how to handle this scene, which is incredible in naturalistic terms, but crucial to the development of the play. From the earliest jottings in his notes on the work through to the detailed account of the rehearsals preserved by several young members of the company we can observe the evolution of staging devices which developed into images of striking and complex theatrical power. Thus in the scene described above, when Cordelia is preparing to oppose Lear, she moves downstage out of this mystical light. As he rejects her, Lear rips the veil in two and throws the separate halves to Goneril and Regan. Left alone at the end of the scene, they pick up and meticulously fold their separate portions like two bourgeois housewives.

The destruction of this unreal fairy-tale world now revealed, in the harsh light which was thrown on it, a bare wilderness, a flat stretch of wasteland. Strehler describes it as 'an empty expanse of earth and mud, lit with shafts of light'. And there is more:

The setting: a theatre/a world. A theatre space which becomes a world; a circus/a world. A circus ring, a cosmic ring for the dramatisation of life and of history. An empty setting: abandoned. Its surface is bleak, muddy, primordial; it is hard work walking on it; your feet sink in it; you get covered in mud when you fall. The precarious dominion of the powerful is laid out by the servants on this land: as fragile as planks over an abyss, or those which are used by clowns or acrobats for balancing acts or death-defying stunts.[20]

The setting had three features: the muddy land, a series of planks, balanced on rostra, and a plain cyclorama at the back. At the end of the play when Lear makes his final entrance the cyclorama was slit open, the head of Cordelia protruded through it and was followed by Lear carrying her in his arms. The image was overwhelming and complex: initially that of birth (a savage irony after the previous rebirth of the father in the arms of his daughter), and subsequently that of an overgrown child desperately playing with a broken doll, a marionette whose limbs hung limp and lifeless.

'Right up to the great scene with the three madmen' – says Eduardo Fadini – 'the story is narrated through the basic image of clowning. The actors teeter on three planks arranged as a bridge over the sawdust of the circus ring: these planks can be a raft or a prison, but they remain the planks of a circus on which trained dogs, clowns, animal tamers and dancers perform their acts.'[21] Shakespeare's imagery – both that relating to savage beasts and that concerned with 'this great stage of fools' – was Strehler's starting point. But the physical images chosen were as polyvalent as the verbal: Lear and Gloucester wore costumes of some ancient world, yet appropriate for clowns (their faces were painted white), whilst the savage younger generation were dressed in tight-fitting black leather. Fadini concludes: 'We seem to be watching a conflict between wild animals (Lear and Gloucester) and their tamers, a play about clowns (the old men) and deranged black-shirts.' The richness of signification in the stage imagery reached its fullest expression in the doubling of the Fool and Cordelia.

The part was performed by an actress, Ottavia Piccolo, who played Cordelia in a conventional manner, but whose Fool was a highly original conception. This was no traditional court jester but a combination of Chaplin, Pierrot and some wild and naughty schoolchild. She had a painted face, red nose and close-cropped hair and wore baggy trousers, a green sequinned tail-coat and an old misshapen top hat. In his notes Strehler compares the character's nature and function with those of Arlecchino. Whilst Arlecchino is clearly male (his lover is Smeraldina) and makes scurrilous jokes, he remains outside the action, uninvolved: 'His troubles and his happiness are short-lived, sudden, like his tantrums, like everything he does. This comic character is incapable of suffering – or suffers all the time – thanks to the contradictions implicit in his fixed but ever-changing role.' Lear's Fool, by contrast, he finds ageless and sexless (it is no surprise to find him debating whether Shakespeare's original Fool, the clown Robert Armin, did actually double the role of Cordelia). More significantly it is the dual nature of the character which he finds disturbing: the 'sweet and bitter fool'. By having the same actress play both Cordelia and the Fool he made sense of the mysterious disappearance of the latter – who returns as the comforting daughter, only to be murdered. Lear's line 'and my poor fool is hanged', addressed to the corpse of Cordelia, clinched the issue. The fool, part conscience, part tormentor, is – through his link with Cordelia – a precarious hold on humanity during the storm. Lombardo describes Piccolo's performance as follows:

She is the unforgettable clown with cropped hair and painted face, alternately comic and tragic, tender and cruel, fragile but the same time strong, happy and sad, full of laughter and desperate: a formidably accomplished performer who conveys all the aspects of the character. Through the clarity of her expression and movement she makes sense of the virtually untranslatable language Shakespeare gives the character, and, above all, elucidates – with that clear direct voice of hers – the truth behind all appearances which is the Fool's *raison d'être*, and – at the same time – the crux of the tragedy.[22]

In his early production notes Strehler reveals himself unsure of how to stage the storm. Should he use sound and lighting effects? music? Peter Brook in his celebrated staging in 1962 had simply lowered metal thunder sheets in full view of the audience: a stark effect but a far cry from Strehler's method. He eventually hit on a powerful and original idea. At the end of the first act Goneril and Regan go indoors with their husbands, leaving Lear shut out as the storm is brewing. They stood in the centre of the stage on a rostrum, whilst the servants raised the wooden planks vertically so as to enclose the

11   Tino Carrara as Lear and Ottavia Piccolo as the Fool, 1972

figures in a wooden case: they were liked caged animals, precariously clinging to their territory, and – as Agostino Lombardo points out – like the Vices of the medieval morality play who have expelled the Virtues from the castle. Act II opened with the curtain down: suddenly it was violently shaken as behind it the audience glimpsed the full paraphernalia of a stage storm during the brief scene between Kent and the Gentleman. As soon as Lear and the Fool appeared, a blinding flash of light was frozen and held throughout the subsequent scenes. The noise stopped, and from then on the whole storm appeared to be taking place within Lear's mind.

For Strehler the play, though confronting extremes of evil and suffering, is in no sense nihilistic. A revealing scene was the blinding of Gloucester – staged with grim realistic force, with Gloucester tied to the planks by ropes and his head pulled back, whilst his tormentors took a sadistic delight in the act. Throughout the torture Gloucester (Renato de Carmine) did not howl or shout, but on learning of Edmund's treachery he emitted a terrible scream: for Strehler the emphasis was on the process of learning rather than the presentation of the cruelty. For this reason Edgar is a crucial figure. In rehearsals Strehler delineated seven separate roles that Edgar plays in the course of the drama. The first six he defines as: faithful elder son, Poor Tom, the 'voice' guiding Gloucester, the peasant who finds Gloucester at the foot of the cliff, the ruffian who kills Oswald, and the unknown knight who kills Edmund. It is his experience in handling these – a sort of Pirandellian 'game of roles' – which makes him able to assume responsibility at the end of the play, a more confident, mature, and human figure: his seventh and final transformation. Strehler was fortunate in having the young Gabriele Lavia, the actor who has since established himself as Italy's leading *mattatore*, to play this role; he rose to the challenge of the part, most notably in the scene in the hovel where his combination of epileptic, knowing fool and simpleton gave added depth to this confrontation of three 'madmen'. More importantly Lavia was called on to sustain the play's ending, which Strehler slightly – but crucially – altered. Instead of the final couplet:

> The eldest hath borne most; we that are young
> Shall never see so much nor live so long.

Edgar had:

> Noi che siamo giovani
> non permetteremo
> che si vedano piu simili sventure
> ne pretenderemo di essere eterni.

('We that are young will not permit such tragic events to occur again nor assume that we will live for ever'): the inevitable conclusion to Strehler's researches into the play's meaning.

Strehler also changed the opening. He cut the initial scene between Kent, Gloucester and Edmund, having Carraro begin the play by making a powerful solo entrance, and, with a gesture of outstretched arms, summon the court to announce his decision to abdicate. For the critic Tullio Kezich this had an autobiographical reference: to Strehler's departure from the Piccolo in

1968 and his return after a turbulent four years as a sadder and wiser man. Strehler's break with the Piccolo had been on political grounds and marked the climax of that process of revaluation which many Italian artists and intellectuals had undertaken. When Strehler returned to the Piccolo with *Lear* he had behind him not only his Brecht stagings and the influence they in turn had exercised on his two previous Shakespeare productions, but the full implications of the direction in which his artistic and political questioning had led him. Lunari says that the most important challenge was the fact that *Lear* has a setting outside history. The specific historical circumstances which determine the development of the events in *Coriolanus* and the Henry VI plays were particularly congenial to Strehler's dialectical mode of research; with *Lear* he was faced with 'the thing itself'. The most striking feature of the production was its simplicity: the simplicity of complex material expounded with clarity. 'This', argues Lunari, 'was the result of a minutely detailed analysis and demolition of the text with the complementary reconstruction and synthesis of its elements, a process which is able to make sense of its contradictions, turn every problem into a meaningful integration of con-trasted viewpoints and translate the obscurities of the text into a dramatic language which is in no way unclear merely because it is difficult to define in words.'[23] Strehler's achievement lay in giving expression to the complexity of ideas through visual and physical images which were not ambiguous but *ambivalent*. This was his inheritance from Brecht, who had taught him that an ability to create clear but resonant stage images – his concept of gestic acting – can translate an ethical and political dialectic into theatrical practice.

The step from *Lear* (1972) to *The Tempest* (1978) was in some sense inevitable. Though Strehler had produced the play before – at the very beginning of his career in very different circumstances and in a very different setting – it is not surprising to find him returning to it after *Lear*. Shakespeare's final plays – the romances, from *Pericles* through to *The Tempest* – take up those issues central to *Lear*. Strehler's decision to restage the play is significant. He has often spoken of the 'need' to do plays; the 'need' to re-stage the same play is a pointer to a particularly strong feeling about the work and its relevance both to his own interests and to those he perceives to be fundamental to his prospective audience. It is a scandal that this – of all Strehler's productions – has not been seen in Britain. Whilst being a fundamentally clear, ungimmicky interpretation of the traditional values of the play, the production is a milestone in twentieth-century stagings because of its ingenious and inspired solutions to so many of the play's theatrical challenges. It is not only a great production of *The Tempest*; it is living proof of how to employ the fullest theatrical means to convey – with extreme simplicity – the complexity of meaning in a familiar and acknowledged masterpiece. If Philip Hope-Wallace was correct in attributing to the Strehler *Arlecchino* a wide influence on theatrical staging in Europe, how much more would *The Tempest* have inspired modern young directors and designers? Let us hope they made the effort to go to Milan.

The Tempest is in effect Shakespeare's final *gioco dei potenti*. It is a play about power: about political power, the force of love, the occult and – perhaps most significantly for Strehler – the power of art in general and theatre in particular to influence people. The theatrical metaphor central to the play – of Prospero the inventor of masques, the 'presenter' of the entertainment, in control of his spirits who act the roles allotted them for the purposes of delusion, terror or celebration in turn – encompasses all the implications of the work: from the political to the comic. Central to Strehler's production was a powerful and complex recourse to theatrical magic. This, appropriately enough, was (in terms of staging) the exact opposite of his *Lear*, with its barren plain, its mud and its planks. Every effort was made in *The Tempest* to astonish and overwhelm the audience, who, like the characters temporarily disarmed by Prospero's own theatrical tricks, were trapped for three hours in a space governed by magic. Strehler's own conclusions as to the limited efficacity of this magic (his own as well as Prospero's) constituted the most challenging feature of his production, and went one stage further than those reached during the course of his researches on and into *Lear*.

On entering the theatre the audience was faced with a thin veil or cloth entirely covering the stage. In front of the raised proscenium (the play was produced not at the Piccolo but at the Lirico, a much larger theatre in Milan) was a sort of orchestra pit. It was empty and consisted of three rows divided by wooden flats. Blue silk could be seen partially draped over the front of this structure. The lights did not fade to blackout; the house was suddenly plunged into pitch darkness (the Italian theatre does not suffer the curse of obligatory house-lights), and 'a tempestuous noise of thunder and lightning' was heard (following precisely Shakespeare's stage directions). The audience saw in front of them – the view from the front stalls was terrifying – what appeared to be a huge (life-size) galleon tossing on a blue ocean. The effect was the perfect modern equivalent of what Inigo Jones produced in some of his court masques, such as *The Masque of Blackness* (1605), in which the opening scene represented a sea in motion. Strehler achieved this by different means, but the intention was to impress the audience and – for a few moments – encourage them to suspend disbelief. The sea in Strehler's production was produced by the efforts of twenty-one stage hands inside the orchestra-pit structure manipulating a vast sheet of blue silk so as to create the impression of waves rising and falling, threatening to engulf the ship. As the noise (produced by percussion offstage) increased it mingled with the shouts of the crew and court caught up in this tempest. Violent flashes of lightning appeared to be the only source of illumination: everything was witnessed in these swift bursts. At the climax of the scene the ship's mast split in two (the comment of the terrified crew 'We split, we split' being given literal theatrical representation) and everything was lost in a slow fade. At the same time the silk, representing the waves, was slowly pulled under the stage, giving the impression of water receding.

This occasioned a great round of applause, at the end of which we found ourselves looking at a man and a girl together in the centre of a wooden island. Sand covered the ground and here and there a shell or small metal object could be glimpsed. The applause was necessary: it acknowledged the effectiveness of the theatrical illusion. Our disbelief had been suspended, but we now acknowledged that the tempest was a magical one; 'not a hair perished': it had all been the result of a conjuring trick. Thus Strehler established at the start his own identification with Prospero: with the director as magician. Here the association of Prospero with Shakespeare (can anyone seriously doubt the valedictory tone of the work?) took on a new lease of life with Strehler, as director, completing the trinity. This allowed him in some respects to bring together and sum up the most important of his theatrical preoccupations – the Pirandellian concern with theatre within theatre; the Brechtian analysis of politics; the *lazzi* of the commedia dell'arte; his lyrical operatic stagings – and employ them in such a way as to throw the different (and contrasted) issues of the play into a new theatrical light whilst at the same time giving them coherence and unity.

After the storm there follows one of the longest scenes in Shakespeare – a scene of calm narration (broken only by Prospero's emotional distress in recalling the terrible events of the past). Tino Carraro played this scene with the consummate skill of the Brechtian actor telling the story, talking (and acting) in the third person, employing the skill most vital to epic acting: that of sustaining a clear gripping narrative. At the end of this Prospero puts Miranda to sleep and invokes Ariel. The audience was due for a further Strehlerian revelation: the appearance of Ariel from the flies, hanging from a clearly visible wire. This gestic effect made clear from the start the relationship between Prospero and Ariel, between this master and servant. It was an emblem characterising the relationship between director and actor: often one of deep mutual love and trust, of gratitude for the freedom given the performer, but also of resentment, of the will to be free and independent. The sheer hard work that goes into theatrical performance was underlined here and made to complement the image Shakespeare creates of a sort of idealised servitude. When Ariel wants to be free he/she (the part was played by one of Strehler's favourite actresses, Giulia Lazzarini) tugged at the wire, which refused to budge. Lazzarini was dressed as a clown, with white face, a sort of sad Pierrot, full of tricks on the ground, who also – when she forgot her servitude – was capable of executing amazing balletic and acrobatic movements high in the air, yet fully able to swoop down suddenly and embrace her master.

Strehler's representation of Ariel – an extraordinarily original achievement in the context of the play's theatrical history – was matched by his portrayal of Caliban. Prospero/Carraro took off his thick leather belt ready to confront the 'slave . . . who never yields us kind answer'. A roaring sound was heard under the stage, a trap-door was flung apart and slowly Caliban appeared. First one long arm, then another, emerged from the hole in the ground and slowly a black shape crawled into view: something between an ape and a dangerous reptile. He remained in shadow well downstage, merely answering Prospero's commands with insults; but then he moved slowly into the light as he recalled Prospero's usurpation of the island, raised himself to full height and slowly turned to confront his master. His huge bright eyes were those of a young boy; his face and (virtually naked) body, seen for the first time, those of a handsome young man. (The two actors who alternated this role, Michele Placido and Massimo Foschi, are noted for their good looks.) Prospero, his belt raised threateningly, now looked the true savage. This was another gestic effect of striking force. Here was the director of *Coriolanus* and *Lear* exploiting to the full the theatrical potential of the play's dialectic. Here was a realisation of the most complex political aspect of the drama, in which Caliban is seen as a devil in the context of the opposition of black and white magic, but as a far more sympathetic figure in the context of another pervasive theme, colonisation. His treatment by Prospero prepares us for the way he is to be handled by Stephano and Trinculo as well as for Antonio's wry comment when he sees him at the end of the play. Strehler's experience in Brechtian staging is particularly evident in his approach to Caliban, whose ambiguity was conveyed throughout the production by precise observation of his physical movement and behaviour in relation to the other figures.

When he meets Trinculo and Stephano subsequently, we are introduced to another level of theatrical reference. The comic scenes of the play present a very special challenge to the modern director. They are neither particularly witty nor original; though they are an important variation on the master–servant/freedom–bondage theme and a strong comment on the recurrent motif of colonisation, they in no way appear to advance the story. Few British directors have had much success with them, the recourse to music hall traditions being a very limited approach to the problem. In making the characters of Trinculo and Stephano figures from the commedia dell'arte

Strehler at once solved the issue, whilst integrating the scenes into the wider theatrical metaphor of the play and production. In the first (Boboli) *Tempest* Strehler had made them respectively Pulcinella and Brighella figures; now, with his wealth of experience of commedia production, he was able to expand this, inventing new *lazzi* to match the ones in the original play. His handling of these scenes strongly supports the theory that they were based on commedia scenarios and that – far from relying on verbal dexterity in interpretation – they require physical skills and improvisation. The mistaking of Caliban and Trinculo under the gabardine for a monster, and the beating Trinculo undergoes through the mischievousness of Ariel cry out for the inspired bravura of commedia.

The first comic scene (Act II scene 2) – the meeting of Caliban, Trinculo and Stephano – is a fine illustration of Strehler's method. Having established the dual nature of Caliban in his first scene with Prospero, Strehler goes on to explore this further. The scene opens with Caliban entering stage right dragging a huge tree trunk on his back; he drops it on hearing the first thunder and runs to hide under the wooden floor which has been raised upstage left. When he emerges he is seen to be a very different figure from the noble savage we have glimpsed in the second scene of the play. He is wearing his 'gabardine' – a coarse black garment which covers his back, also forming a hood to frame his face, which is now sporting war-paint. He is brandishing a stick to which are attached totemic shells and he now speaks with a gruff, harsh voice. As he curses Prospero he crouches, legs apart, arms spread; then, pounding out a savage rhythm, he draws magical circles in the sand which he then rubs ritualistically on his face. We are observing the son of Sycorax here: in the context of the theme of colonisation Caliban is noble and wronged; but in the context of magic he is primitive and dangerous.

On hearing another thunderclap he runs downstage, gibbering hysterically and shaking; then he crouches on all fours, covered from head to foot in the gabardine. Trinculo enters upstage right. He has a high-pitched voice and his vowels are elongated and distorted with a heavy Neapolitan accent. He wears the costume of Pulcinella – white baggy shirt and trousers and a cone-shaped white hat. He is the clown of the scene, endlessly inventive in his gestures. When he addresses the cloud Strehler adds the first of many interpolated passages extending the original text, which is treated with the freedom of a commedia scenario. A second cloud is introduced, chatted to and then dismissed as Trinculo turns to 'quella incinta' (the pregnant one), a description he underlines with a broad comic gesture. He then sits on Caliban by mistake, jumps up, lifts the gabardine and – staring at his backside – pronounces this 'a man'. He pushes Caliban over with his foot and then begins a matador routine, preparing to taunt the 'monster' with his red cloak.

The Neapolitan Pulcinella thinks of taking his monster back – not to England, but to Milan (where the money is) – and does an impression of a fairground barker (with exaggeratedly deep voice) advertising his prize attraction ('venite avanti, accomodatevi': 'come on, roll up, roll up!' he improvises). He lifts up Caliban's toes tentatively and counts them, comparing the number with his own. When another thunder-clap is heard he throws the cloak over his head, only to panic thinking it has gone dark. He then crawls through Caliban's arms and remains crouching under him, facing the other way.

The plethora of gags and inventions typifies Trinculo. By contrast Stephano is not funny. He is very drunk, has a loud hoarse voice and is first seen making his way through the empty 'orchestra pit' which serves to support the blue silk representing the sea. As the 'monster' scuttles backwards and forwards downstage Stephano stands upstage, throws his cloak over his shoulder, puffs out his chest and tries to stand firm and defiant. He strikes the pose of the braggart captain (a role he will assume more fully in his next scene) though he is costumed here as Brighella, the most villainous of the commedia clowns, in white with the distinctive barred pattern on his jacket. He is from the North – later when Trinculo shouts 'two Neapolitans scap'd!' he retorts 'I'm from the Veneto, actually' – and when he thinks of profiting from the monster Strehler has him think of taking it to Naples (in the exploited – and uneducated – South).

The political themes of the play find a fresh focus here, which is thrown into even sharper ironic relief with the subsequent adoration of Stephano by Caliban. As Trinculo, perched precariously on top of the wooden flats of the 'orchestra' in front of the stage, laughs at the scene, Stephano's savage drunken behaviour contrasts with the mellifluous quality Caliban's voice now assumes and the unexpected grace of his movements. Here Caliban appears a child, lost in this company, bewildered by the drink, rolling his head slowly as he offers to serve Stephano. The speech beginning 'I prithee let me bring thee where crabs grow' is choreographed with the utmost beauty and precision. Caliban is now seated cross-legged; he rubs his arms together, pressing them against his cheek as he begs to assist Stephano; then his fingers stretch out and unfold gently as he talks of digging up the 'pig nuts'; his right arm extends slowly in the air at the mention of the 'jay's nest', moves over to the left to capture the 'marmoset', then both hands climb above the head to reach for the 'clustering filberts', and he ends the speech with his arms fully outstretched at an angle of forty-five degrees.

The three characters are defined by their vocal tone and physical appearance. Caliban's voice and bearing both change radically during the scene: an alienation effect which alerts the audience to the shift of perspective. The studied precision of movement – which has all the force of the Brechtian *Gestus* – goes alongside the inventiveness in the improvisation so as to explore the paradox of acting (keeping a balance between what is set/repeated and what is fresh/invented) which is basic to the commedia dell'arte.

If there is one criticism that can be levelled against the production – and it was one brought by the Polish critic Jan Kott, whose writing had influenced the staging and who was invited to attend rehearsals in Milan – it is that Strehler minimised the dangers to Prospero throughout. He was too much in control. Certainly Trinculo and Stephano never presented any real threat – which in a sense becomes a problem when Prospero, having 'forgot the foul conspiracy of the beast Caliban and his confederates against (my) life', is so disturbed by this revelation that the magic of the masque he has created for Ferdinand and Miranda disappears as the spirits 'heavily vanish'. The limited force of his magic and the recognition of his all-too-human weakness of forgetfulness (a disturbing reminder of what had happened in Milan when he was too 'wrapt in secret studies') was underplayed in this production, which dispensed with the masque altogether. Moreover, in the scene of the attempt on the sleeping Alonzo's life (again, this can be interpreted as a chilling parallel with the two attempts on Prospero's), Strehler introduced a highly original effect which served to emphasise the power of Prospero. Instead of merely lulling the court asleep with the music, Ariel threw a handful of sand in each person's eyes in turn, thus converting the musical image into a more powerfully visual and theatrical gesture, but he left Sebastian and Antonio alone, thereby informing us that the plot was foreseen by Prospero and in his control. This fitted Strehler's conception of the nature of Prospero's power; but it does detract from the play's dramatic tension if the protagonist is virtually all-powerful. Yet we were scarcely conscious of any fight against time on Prospero's part, since the production lasted well over three hours (even with the masque excised) and had a deliberate, slow-motion, elegiac pace.

These criticisms are unimportant in a production which so fully grounded the ethical and political themes of the play in theatrical images. This was evident in all the scenes between Prospero and Ariel, particularly those at the end of the play. When the 'three men of sin' are presented with the consequences of their actions as the banquet disappears and Ariel enters as a harpy, a powerful *coup de théâtre* occurred. The stage went dark, the waves (of blue silk) rose again, threatening to engulf the characters, and in flashes of lightning Ariel descended from the flies, screeching, with beak and talons ready to tear the courtiers apart. But the most stunning – and most meaningful – effect was reserved to the end. Prospero, having freed Ariel, lifted his wand high between his hands and snapped it in two. As he did so the whole of the 'orchestra pit' collapsed, flies and drapes fell on the stage and a heavy partition clumsily descended, covering most of the platform. Theatrical art and stage illusion were destroyed as surely as the actor's cart had been by the metal screen which fell in Strehler's production of *The Mountain Giants*. But this was not the final act; Shakespeare's hope for the future 'brave new world', not Pirandello's despair, was the subject. There remained the epilogue as Prospero finally, and humbly, begs the audience for its forgiveness and indulgence. The acknowledgement of this – applause – caused an even greater theatrical miracle to occur: the stage reassembled before our eyes, whilst Ariel – who had run off through the auditorium – came back on stage to join her master.

The significance of the production in general and this finale in particular was summed up by Strehler:

Here, at the heart of *The Tempest*, the man of the theatre finds himself face to face with the ultimate reality of theatre. He touches – or thinks he touches – the most extreme limits of theatre. In *The Tempest* there is the most pronounced sense of the weariness and vanity of theatre and at the same time the glorification both of theatre and of life. The mistaken yet triumphant glorification of theatre as the finest expression of consciousness and history, but a limited means, never fully capable of capturing the inexplicable workings of life. Life that is theatre, but at every moment is more than theatre. Great courage, desperate courage is needed to stage Shakespeare's *Tempest* today. But perhaps we need just such gestures now ... *The Tempest* seems at this time, above all else – and its themes are vast: politics, history, art, theatre – to dramatise a path of self-discovery on the part of its protagonist, Prospero, towards the conquest of reality, and therefore represents a difficult path of self-discovery for us, the interpreters, and for you, the audience. But above all else it is a huge metaphor of theatre. Alongside the profound questions concerning life itself, history and the problem of understanding that Shakespeare poses, there are also questions about the destiny of theatre itself. That is, questions about how and why we create theatre – we, people working in theatre – and about what theatre should or could be.[23]

5   Brecht stopped at Milan

The work of demystification we are pursuing in capitalist countries is the direct result of epic theatre and particularly of Brecht's theatre ... here in Italy it is a pressing matter. Even those who are well-versed in dialectical materialism – or those who should be – are victims of Marxism. Because bourgeois society knows how to direct its propaganda. Our job is to identify the problems – with the help of epic theatre, rational theatre, committed theatre (as against uncommitted theatre, negative theatre, the theatre of the capitalist system) and to show that the world needs to be changed and can be changed. It isn't enough to show how the world is changing; you must also show what mankind can and must do to change the world.

Strehler in Del 'classico' B.B., ed. Arturo Lazzari, p. 93

'Brecht si è fermato a Milano' ('Brecht stopped at Milan') was the punchline of a sketch by the Italian singer and comedian Luigi Proietti in a review in 1984. Playing on the title of the celebrated book by Carlo Levi – and film by Francesco Rosi – *Cristo si è fermato ad Eboli* (*Christ Stopped at Eboli*), it was a mordant comment both on Strehler's championing of the dramatist and on the relative neglect of his work in Italy. Strehler was not the first person to direct Brecht in Italy, and he was certainly not the last, but his approach is unique, being born of an intense love of the work (one which deepened through his brief friendship with the writer) which has expressed itself through an exhaustive attempt to explore the implications and potential of epic theatre.

Strehler came to Brecht relatively late in his career. This was a conscious decision; production of his work had been announced for the Piccolo several years before *The Threepenny Opera* was performed there in 1956 (this work and *Mother Courage* being the two works Strehler had been thinking of mounting for some time), but Strehler continued to put off his confrontation with the author until preparations began in earnest in 1955 for a staging of *The Threepenny Opera*.

The delay was significant and points to an awareness from the start that Brecht represented a unique challenge. This was twofold. In the first place, an exploration of historical drama (in the plays of Shakespeare) and of the realistic canon (resulting in the productions of *The Cherry Orchard* and *El nost Milan* in 1955) led inevitably to Brecht. In discussing this with Ugo Ronfani, Strehler points out that his work on Shakespeare had helped him to understand the theatricality of Brecht's plays better, and that *El nost Milan*'s status as popular theatre had affinities with Brecht. Indeed, his consideration of *The Threepenny Opera* in the period prior to his first staging of the work influenced that early production of the Bertolazzi, notably in his approach to the opening scene of *El nost Milan*, set in Tivoli. And when he first discussed staging *The Threepenny Opera* he considered the advantages of transferring the piece to a Milanese setting, an idea which he subsequently abandoned.

Secondly, the fact that Strehler had for some time been considering *The Threepenny Opera* and *Mother Courage* – two very different pieces, one from Brecht's early period and the other a mature work – points to his concern with the other aspect of the challenge: the need to find the right play to appeal to an Italian audience. Though he had for some time considered the leading role in *Mother Courage* as a fitting challenge for Lilla Brignon he finally settled for *The Threepenny Opera* as the work with which an Italian audience could more readily identify. It had a particular appeal for Strehler himself and for the generation who had lived through the war: its songs were familiar and the subversive quality of the whole piece lent it a weight of emotional significance. For Strehler, the director, it represented what he has termed an act of 'polemical aggression' against the naturalistic theatre on the one hand and the expressionist *Urschrei* on the other. It is interesting that Strehler firmly rejects any expressionist features of the work, emphasising instead its political satire and its employment of techniques from popular theatre. He regards the most positive feature of the piece as its contradictions which open up the dialectic of the drama, arguing that:

the ambiguity of *The Threepenny Opera* will create a sense of uncertainty, of unease in the bourgeois public for whom it is performed. The laughs must be hesitant, consciously or unconsciously critical. Whether the audience is aware of it or not, the play will make them think and take action . . . for this reason there is a profound justification for performing *The Threepenny Opera* – today.[1]

Strehler, however, was very shrewd in choosing a work which, whilst it fulfilled the polemical aims of epic theatre, employed a variety of dramatic devices consonant with Brecht's concept of *Spass*, or fun: devices which give the piece its fundamental appeal as entertainment. Strehler saw these features as important for both the audience and the actors, unfamiliar with Brecht's drama, as a means to assimilate the techniques and aims of epic theatre:

The appealing theatrical techniques – from opera, revue, cabaret and cinema – despite their inherent dangers, can, within certain limits, become helpful starting points for the performers, assisting them in discovering an epic style . . . these same dangerously fascinating features of the work are the theatrical devices which *assault* the audience in an enjoyable way . . . *The Threepenny Opera* challenges the public and makes its ideological criticism through entertaining, purely 'gastronomic' techniques – of irony and comic analogy. It is our job to make sure that the mere fascination of the setting, the apparent sympathy for the characters, the pleasure of the melodies, the savage anarchy of the verbal satire don't just become ends in themselves . . . but, at the same time, we mustn't suffocate the bursting poetic vitality of the text in critical and ideological commitment.[2]

Though the precise political significance of the piece has shifted through Strehler's three productions – in 1956, 1973 and 1986 respectively – *The Threepenny Opera* has revealed itself as the key to the director's skill in presenting the work of Brecht as both appealing and meaningful theatre for an Italian – and subsequently a wider European – audience.

Strehler's biographers rightly emphasise the significance of the 1956 production of *The Threepenny Opera* as a landmark in his career and in the development of the Italian theatre; both Ronfani and Guazzotti stated (incorrectly – see below) that prior to this production only two stagings of Brecht had been seen in Italy, both of them in 1953: *Man is Man*, directed by Gianfranco De Bosio at the Teatro Ruzzante in Padua, and *Mother Courage*, directed by Luciano Lucignani at the Satiri in Rome. Both critics emphasise also that these productions were essentially experimental, academic exercises which had little or no influence on Brecht's reputation in Italy. Strehler had in fact got his own experimental staging out of the way before he tackled *The Threepenny Opera*: he had undertaken a production of the one-act *Lehrstück: Die Massnahme* with students from the Piccolo school. This had only one performance, and Strehler has drawn attention to its significance for him by stating that these didactic pieces were intended by Brecht not – as is commonly and erroneously believed – as scripts to 'train the public' in the techniques of epic theatre, but rather as exercises which actors – and directors – can employ to study these devices and put them into practice. Just as Stanislavski was to warn exponents of the American Method (including Joshua Logan, who visited him in Moscow in 1930) that some of his more celebrated exercises were 'for the bathroom, not to be exposed in public', so the more nakedly experimental aspects of the epic technique were initially studied by Strehler in the relative privacy of his acting school.

It is interesting that neither Ronfanin or Guazzotti mentions the fact that Strehler was not the first to produce *The Threepenny Opera* in Italy. The work had in fact been staged in 1929 (a year after the Berlin premiere) by the pioneer director Anton Giulio Bragaglia, a member of the futurist movement whose eclectic tastes rivalled those of Strehler, and who had founded his experimental Teatro degli Indipendenti in Rome in the mid-twenties. When the Piccolo production played in Rome in May 1956 Bragaglia was not slow to point out that he had preceded Strehler by twenty-seven years. His tetchy article (published in *Film d'Oggi*) is worth quoting at length since he himself, in explaining how he directed the piece and in stating what for him are its dramatic strengths, serves to underline the innovatory aspect of Strehler's production. Bragaglia's approach is typical of the emphasis Strehler wished at all cost to avoid: a refusal to address the political issues of the piece or to relate the epic to the 'gastronomic' features. Bragaglia confessed that his enthusiasm for the work was based on its 'highly original satire of English opera conventions, the Villon-inspired songs added by Brecht, Weill's music and Brecht's culinary skills' – which, he adds – 'seemed marvellous yesterday though today they appear less so because no longer new'. He points out:

I quite simply pruned the Marxist sallies and thus did the public a service by making sure they wouldn't be bored by them. The socialists like Grassi and Strehler dedicate their evening of anti-bourgeois insults to the wealthy who alone can pay the high prices demanded by these elitist shows. It is merely a sign of bad breeding to insult the paying public who support the company; the venomous satire in Brecht's play is of interest only to the Marxists.[3]

When Strehler's third production opened in Paris in 1986, the critic Ugo Volli questioned the motives of the wealthy and fashionable Parisian audience who were applauding Brecht's satire, concluding that Strehler 'had from the start taken for granted that his audience would be deaf to the piece's ideology and had contented himself with giving them a perfect and desperate theatrical portrait of themselves, a nihilistic insult, the sign of something lacking: perhaps, indeed, the presence of Brecht'.[4] Bragaglia put his finger on a vexed issue: that of performing works whose ideological content does not correspond with the views and lifestyle of the audience. He adds that the critic Renato Simoni 'observed that I had cut the Marxist gibes because they annoyed the bourgeois public and were particularly irritating to a reactionary like myself. Every director mounts the production he wants to, bearing in mind the tastes and requirements of the audience it is aimed at.' Strehler has always maintained that Brecht's theatre is uncomfortable: he was aware that his first production of *The Threepenny Opera* had offended many people. 'The middle-class public reacted to *The Threepenny Opera* as though they'd been hit in the stomach', whilst Brecht's admirers on the far left were distressed to discover that 'in order to be revolutionary, theatre must be beautiful'. 'They discovered above all', he adds, 'that reality is a matter of dialectic, the opposite of their mummified Marxism.'[5] What mattered to Strehler was that those members of the audience with an open mind and a sense of curiosity had understood: 'they realised that intolerance and dogmatism had nothing to do with Brecht but characterised the attitude of his enemies'.

Here we can glimpse most clearly Strehler's social and political motivation. His attitude is very close to that of Edward Bond, who uses familiar and entertaining dramatic forms (comedy of manners, naturalistic domestic drama, cartoon-style humour) in a subversive way in order to shake and challenge the audiences ideology. Bond, too, has been very strongly influenced by Brecht and he shares Strehler's insistence on the fundamentally humane and rational significance of theatre. Strehler's argument concerning the relationship between entertainment and didacticism illustrates the marked similarities between them:

Essentially there are two approaches: you either start with what is pleasant from a visual, physical, aural point of view and gradually add the acid drop by drop as required. Or you start with what is unpleasant or disturbing and juggle this with the pleasant, the attractive, the magical.[6]

Strehler points out that in his first staging of *The Threepenny Opera* he took the first approach; it was in preparing the second (1973) that he formulated the theory quoted above and indeed attempted in that version to approach the work from the alternative point of view in order to make the production more 'provocative'. An examination of his three stagings reveals a consistent, yet developing, approach to Brecht, whose theory and practice have continued increasingly to influence the whole corpus of Strehler's work.

Before mounting *The Threepenny Opera* he had read and analysed Brecht's work with a devouring enthusiasm. Brecht is his third 'maestro', more important than either Jouvet or Copeau: their teaching was restricted essentially to theatrical practice, whilst from Brecht he learned a more complex and significant social and political ideology. Towards the end of his lengthy essay in *Per un teatro umano* he reveals his debt to Brecht and his belief in the importance of his work:

Brecht didn't just leave us his plays, he left us a very complex method; he revealed to us a direction we could take. As far as epic theatre is concerned we won't achieve a complete, in-depth production. We're in the process of discovering a teaching method, for actors on the one hand and for directors on the other. Therefore we're only at the beginning, the first stage of true epic theatre. We're still only pupils and it seems to me typical (and ridiculous) that whilst we know we've scarcely begun our work, others believe that epic theatre is out of date and we should be exploring other approaches. From a theoretical point of view only now, after the recent publication of Brecht's complete works, can we fully realise that there really are a lot of problems still to be solved.[7]

At the time of stating this (1968) Strehler had already tackled *The Threepenny Opera*, *The Good Person of Setzuan*, *Schweyk in the Second World War*, *Galileo* and *St Joan of the Stockyards*, but he was able to claim here and elsewhere that he had hardly begun his work on Brecht. In answer to critics who accused him of an excessive interest in the dramatist he was to reply (as he continues to do) that he had undertaken too little, not too much, research into his work. To date he has mounted three different productions of both *The Threepenny Opera* and *The Good Person of Setzuan*, *Schweyk in the Second World War*, *Galileo* and *St. Joan of the Stockyards*, a version of *The Exception and the Rule* staged in a double-bill with Miller's *A Memory of Two Mondays* (1962), Weill's *Mahagonny* and Dessau's *Lucullus* for La Scala (in 1964 and 1973), as well as the evenings of anthologies of Brecht's poetry and songs with Milva. Yet he sees that these shows in the context both of Brecht's output and his own stagings (some 250 to date) are relatively few. The reality is that whilst his interest in Brecht has been a determining factor in his career, the implications of Brecht's theatrical revolution (unprecedented in this century in Strehler's opinion) are out of all proportion to what can be achieved by an interpreter of his work. Moreover, Strehler is the director of the Piccolo Teatro, not of the Berliner Ensemble (a position he declined when it was offered him by Helene Weigel after Brecht's death); Brecht cannot be his sole — or central — focus.

It was just such an awareness of the scope and complexity of Brecht's theatre which caused him to hesitate for so long over the choice of that first production and to mount it with such painstaking care. He went to Berlin to discuss the play with Brecht, armed with a list of twenty-seven very precise questions relating to Brecht's staging of the work in 1928 and to the techniques of epic theatre. Strehler recalls how little Brecht could remember of the original production and his amused delight on observing that Strehler knew far more than he did about it. Strehler had the idea of setting the work in America, rather than the England inherited from Gay's original, and Brecht welcomed this as a more meaningful contemporary reflection of the economic world of the play, suggesting an Italianate New York just after the turn of the century as a telling parallel to his Victorian milieu. Strehler was concerned about the acting techniques and how an Italian company could approach the work:

Strehler asked Brecht's advice as to what you could do about actors who had no conception whatever of what constitutes epic theatre. He asked: 'Is it possible to mount a Brecht work when you have only one actor who understands epic theatre?' and wanted to know if techniques existed that taught you how to act in an epic manner. Brecht reassured Strehler by saying that even his performers acted only to some extent in an epic style: 'It is easier to act in this way in comedy because a strong measure of distancing is essential. The epic style is much easier to understand in this context and so it is advisable to mount comic pieces regularly.' Brecht suggested employing a method he had himself explored: 'the actors have to insert "Brücken-verse" (linking/bridge passages) in their speeches so that they are delivered in the third person, rather like an account: the performer has to add the phrase "he says" after each statement. The problem is that without having recourse to dialectic it is impossible to arrive at the epic.'[8]

Strehler did not attempt in rehearsal to jettison techniques of naturalistic acting, but rather tried to develop and extend them by subjecting them to the scrutiny of a more rational objective approach. Virginio Puecher, who followed the rehearsals and has written an illuminating account of them, tells us that Stanislavski's celebrated demands 'How? Why? and When?' in relation to the characters' actions were not abandoned, but questioned. There were sessions when scenes were performed in a naturalistic way and then discussed with the other actors. Strehler tape-recorded many of the rehearsals and the results were meticulously (sometimes painfully) analysed. He encouraged the actors to follow Brecht's advice and question the immutability of the character. Gradually the pattern of rehearsals changed so that the customary alternation between sudden moments of inspiration and periods of inertia gave way to a more relaxed and productive atmosphere as long discussions of motivation changed to an observation, a narration of character. The actors began to appreciate different values in their performance: entrances, specific objects, the use of the space, changing rhythms emerged as more significant; they began to realise that they could strongly influence the theatrical event.

Strehler has never swerved from his belief that a combination of the techniques of epic theatre and naturalism is basic to a theatre of true dialectic. 'I believe the salvation of modern theatre', he has argued, 'looking at it from a stylistic point of view, is dependent on a synthesis (yet to be achieved) of the two methods of Stanislavski and Brecht.'[9] He further states that his own experience of handling the dialectic of epic theatre resides in 'a synthesis of Stanislavskian realism (without the excesses characteristic of the Actor's Studio) and Italian theatricality (shorn of the outmoded conventions which established themselves in the inter-war period)'.[10] This accounts both for his interest in the features from popular entertainment evident in *The Threepenny Opera* and for his choice of actors. The first production employed two performers from the world of variety: Milly (as Jenny) and Mario Carotenuto (as Peacham). In 1973 Macheath was played – with great success – by the popular singer Domenico Modugno (celebrated throughout Europe on account of the success of the song 'Volare') and Jenny was played by another singer, Milva (who repeated the role in the Paris staging).

The emphasis on the popular side of the work was ratified by Brecht, who came to Milan for the final rehearsals of the 1956 production and attended the first night. Strehler records how he moved silently and with absolute confidence around the darkened auditorium, though when he continued to laugh so loudly at his own work the actors demanded angrily who this friend of Strehler was who insisted on disrupting the rehearsal. Even the director himself was taken off guard when one of the actors, Andrea Matteuzzi (playing Jacob), invented an entirely new piece of business, going offstage at the height of the prison scene in the last act, taking a black armband from his pocket, and returning wearing it to emphasise the fact that Macheath was to all intents and purposes dead. Strehler was enraged, but Brecht rushed on to the stage crying: 'Brilliant! I love it!' Grassi had persistently objected to Strehler's extravagance in requiring a band of a dozen players; now, much to his delight, Brecht remarked regretfully that *he* had had to make do with six.

Brecht loved the Milan staging, as a result of which he entrusted Strehler with the artistic direction of all his works. This request was typed on the back of an envelope which he sent to Strehler after the production had opened. At the final dress rehearsal he also wrote a new ending to the piece, a last verse to the final song expressing a new confidence in humanity which the staging had inspired:

Don't think you're better than the thief or beggar;
Do not accept the fact of poverty.
Keep up instead the fight against injustice
Until the winner is humanity.

In the end Strehler did set the first production in New York, immediately prior to the First World War. The concept of American-style gangsters was therefore basic, and one which recurred in both the later productions: the second was set a little later (in the age of prohibition) and the third alluded to the power of the Mafia. Gags from silent-screen comedy abounded: the policemen who arrest Macheath were dressed like English bobbies and behaved like the Keystone Cops. Another detail of the first production recurred in the others: the scene of Macheath's wedding to Polly took place

12   Brecht – complete with Arlecchino mask and cloth cap – backstage during rehearsals of *The Threepenny Opera*, 1956

not in a stable but in a garage, the matrimonial bed for the couple being provided by opening up the back of a large limousine.

Strehler's understanding of the significance of the *Gestus* in Brecht's work was evident in sequences where the political satire is at it sharpest, sequences whose force has developed with the later productions. One of these was an invention of Strehler's at the end of the first scene of Act III where Peachum's beggars, one after the other, slowly file across the stage in an increasingly horrific exhibition of distress and physical disability, all the more disturbing because it was faked. In the Paris version the scene was described by Roberto De Monticelli as follows:

The intimidating march of the false beggars in the final act is extraordinarily powerful in its violence (as it was in the first production) so much so that the audience remain riveted to their seats and are only capable of venting their feelings through a wild outburst of applause. This third version is even more stylised, each succeeding image standing out on its own, fixed in a precise *Gestus* like a note of music.[11]

By reference to the powerful moment in *Mother Courage* when the dumb Katrin makes the suicidal gesture of drumming to alert the nearby townspeople to the danger of the army, Strehler has explained the importance of this crucial Brechtian device with great clarity:

The *Gestus* is not a matter of aesthetics but of social observation. For Brecht it has ideological connotations and it is meant to disorientate us. Look at Angelika Hurwicz as Katrin. There's more to it than a talented actress miming the role of a dumb girl. We must be made aware of *how* she is miming and *why*; if it's done in one way it's a *Gestus*, if in another it might just be a mimed dance *à la* Jean-Louis Barrault which would be of far less interest to us.[12]

Strehler has praised the skill of Italian performers, which can express itself via a physical brio which is at the furthest extreme from the low-key naturalism favoured by the British actor. This gives the Italian artist an advantage when it comes to playing Brecht, but, as Strehler has also emphasised, this exuberance must be tamed and disciplined so that the resultant physical image is both precise and richly allusive. Another scene in *The Threepenny Opera* illustrates this clearly: the Cannon Song performed by Macheath and Tiger Brown. In Strehler's version Macheath's followers also gradually take part, finally joining in the last chorus. Almost without being aware of it, they take their weapons out of their pockets – razors, chains, knives, pistols; even the priest has one; on the final chord the guns go off: we glimpse fire and smoke, there is a blackout, the group split up as though coming out of a dream, put their weapons away and quietly go back to the wedding celebration. Strehler comments:

By the end of the scene the audience can say that on the one hand they have seen and heard a violent war-song which ends with a chorus, a stunning dramatic crescendo, attractive from a visual point of view (with telling effects such as the group of different people coming together as a chorus and marching as though they were all soldiers). A *coup de théâtre*. On the other hand they have witnessed a demystifying of the mythology of war, an alienation of warlike action, a revelation of the shameful involvement of ordinary people in the crowd of warmongers – even the priest who becomes a bloodthirsty military chaplain, capable of blessing both flags and torturers.[13]

Strehler made these comments when considering the second staging (1973), a version he intended to be more aggressive. The period was shifted to the twenties; the major innovations remained, but they took on an added political sharpness and bite. Massimo Gallerani describes the effect of the Cannon Song in this production:

an angry and bitter progression from the lively brutal cameraderie of army friends through open warmongering to a maudlin drunkenness expressed in a wail for lost youth – when nothing had been lost and you could dare anything; a threatening fascist march, an outburst of colonialism in which the rest of the company – at first in a clandestine, then in a more open way – participate. A mounting explosion of murderous fury which is frozen in the final howl.[14]

Strehler is able to analyse the way this complex gestic effect works on the audience:

The applause bursts out here spontaneously. And its implications are complex. It liberates a variety of tensions aroused by different features: the purely animal, rhythmic (lowest) level of response; the disturbing feelings which need to be exorcised or distanced; the social conscience which has been able to analyse the gang's marching and singing, demystifying their conduct; the aesthetic pleasure of the show, its status as 'good theatre'.[15]

The figure of Macheath is the most complex in the play and the first creator of the role, Tino Carraro, scored a particular success, making it clear that he had mastered the technique of epic acting. Bernard Dort – writing in 1959 – summed up his achievement, making a telling parallel with his Coriolanus:

Mackie is in effect the cornerstone of *The Threepenny Opera*. Strehler and Carraro have made him the eternal romantic brigand, the hero of *The Lower Depths*, thereby running the risk of the play slipping into the realm of sentimental folklore. If on the other hand you stick rigorously to Brecht's description of Mackie as 'a gentleman caught in a delicate emotional situation' and 'the representative of the small middle-class craftsman who is the victim of big business' there is the danger of paralysing the theatrical dialectic of the piece, robbing us of an essential part of its entertainment value. Tino Carraro has created a combination of these two approaches to the character. We have already seen him in *Coriolanus*: having emphasised the arrogance and the blindness of the hero he managed to convey his rare moments of insight and ended by playing him as a wild animal, thus giving us a perfect example of epic acting. He is even better as Mackie: from the start and throughout he shows us both the bandit and the bourgeois. It is impossible to imagine a finer performance: a more bourgeois bandit or a bandit who is more of a bourgeois.[16]

In the second version the part was taken by the popular singer Domenico Modugno, who surprised everyone by his consummate performance of this role. It was again perfect proof of Strehler's belief that you should begin with the popular aspect of the piece and work from there, causing the satire to spring from the song and dance routines, the dialectic to emerge in the conflict of different worlds. Sandro Dini discusses a rehearsal he attended in which the tango with Jenny (Milva) was being rehearsed. Strehler had them dance together and then, when Jenny leaves, Mackie dances alone. Strehler repeated the scene many times, as Modugno had not fully grasped its significance. Finally, he went on to the stage and *demonstrated* what he was after: and herein lies the particular success of his method in directing Brecht. He explained – and showed – that if a man dances alone his loneliness is total, enormous, close to despair; that Mackie, though a rich and successful man, recalls the time with Jenny when he was really happy and this has got under his skin. 'When you dance alone', he explained, 'and now and again you must turn your back to the audience so that they can't perceive your loneliness because they can't see your face, you are quite lost in that memory; the present no longer exists.' Here was a moving alienation effect expressed

13   The Cannon Song in *The Threepenny Opera*, 1973

through a powerful *Gestus*; we are suddenly made to see Mackie from a new angle, to reassess our reactions: this is the Brechtian dialectic at work. Dini tells us that when Modugno began the scene again he was 'quite transformed. He no longer presented the smiling stereotype – the character *he* had seen in the text – but Strehler's Mackie. It was brilliant!'[17]

Strehler's third Mackie was Michael Heltau, the Austrian actor who had worked with him previously in Vienna. The Paris production – performed in French (with the exception of some of the songs) – boasted an international cast. Peachum and his wife were played by distinguished actors from the Comédie-Française, Yves Robert and Denise Gence; Barbara Sukowa, the German film actress, played Polly; and Milva repeated her performance as Jenny. Not all the critics were happy about the result – an extreme step in Strehler's aim to create a genuinely international theatre of Europe – or (as we have noted from Volli's review) convinced of the validity of performing this satirical piece at the Châtelet, a huge theatre, once Diaghilev's base, for a large and fashionable audience. As Gastone Geron pointed out, the setting 'On the Waterfront', where you expected Eddie Carbone to appear at any minute and take a view from the bridge, was the background for a production more grotesque than the previous two. Guido Davico Bonino felt that Strehler was employing the different nationalities of his actors to emphasise the fact that each of the characters 'isolated in his individual loneliness' was 'living in an oppressively nightmare world'. He drew attention to the three main settings: Peachum's 'lobster-red shop', Mackie's 'purple-red garage' and Jenny's 'Chinese-red brothel' which seemed like 'three theatrical mansions, three fixed, static, narrow spaces straight from a medieval mystery play which has been turned on its head, in a stridently blasphemous way'.[18] The element of parody in the miraculous reprieve at the end was exaggerated – the actors dressed like extras from *Norma* and *Aida* – though the employment here of Sicilian puppets in the context of this absurd operatic farrago irresistibly brought to mind the manipulative power of the Cosa Nostra.

The three productions of *The Threepenny Opera* have illustrated Strehler's versatility, his willingness to enter into the dialectic fundamental to the staging of the same work at different points in time. Though his theatrical emphasis has changed, the interrelationship of the contrasted elements of the piece – from broad comedy to savage satire – has demonstrated its essential vitality and validity. In the three decades separating the first production from the last Strehler has undertaken several other Brecht stagings, but the experience in 1956 fully confirmed his belief in the values of Brecht's theatre:

We were interested in Brecht's politics of course, but we were also fascinated by Brecht the dramatic poet. We were convinced that Brecht didn't demean himself by employing theatre as a vulgar method of preaching politics – or as his enemies used to argue – as mere propaganda. We were convinced that the theatricality of his work didn't spring from a dialectic of the mind, artistically forced and unsatisfactory, but from real dramatic situations, from the conflict of characters observed with truth and humanity. The extraordinary success of *The Threepenny Opera* proved that we were not mistaken. That therefore we could go ahead and offer the public other works of a more challenging nature.[19]

This challenge – to take on a more complex work by the mature dramatist – was faced two years later with the first staging of *The Good Person of Setzuan* in 1958. As with *The Threepenny Opera*, this was a play which Strehler was to direct on three separate occasions, though a long gap separated this first staging from the second (in Hamburg in 1977). When he brought the leading actress, Andrea Jonasson, to Milan to perform the play in Italian four years later, both her performance and the production as a whole were essentially the same. The first Milan version was very different; it was much simpler, closer to a traditional Brecht staging: poor theatre to match the fable of poverty and exploitation in China. Siegfried Melchinger, who attended rehearsals of the play, describes the activity of the technicians constructing the scenery:

In the courtyard outside, carpenters are hammering, technicians are working, the scenery is being painted. A world is being created from lightly-charred planks and discoloured tree trunks. At Setzuan there are telegraph poles and a cement factory. The covering which will constitute the floor of the stage will consist of grey tiles made to look like cement. But where the people live the era of industrialisation has not yet begun. They have built their own hovels and made their own poor furniture. They use little wooden carts which they have constructed themselves – a dozen or so of these are strewn around the courtyard. A couple of wooden stools are new but the costumes will be for the most part rags because in the city of Setzuan there is terrible poverty.

The double role of Shen-Te/Shui-Ta was taken by Valentina Fortunato, who in reply to a letter in the theatre magazine *Sipario* explained significantly that though Brecht's dramatic parable required a technique of epic acting, at the same time 'weight must be given to the more traditional – let us say Chekhovian – values'. Undoubtedly Brecht's enthusiasm for the Milanese production of *The Threepenny Opera* encouraged Strehler to take what some directors might regard as a dangerous risk – encouraging a strong element of emotional identification in the performance. Indeed there is a marked disparity between the German and Italian critics of the second production – the former accusing Strehler of sentimentality, the latter welcoming his fusion of realistic and epic theatre – which goes beyond matters of chauvinism. The double role at the centre of the play is tailor-made for Strehler's approach and he has gone on to emphasise all the more the two worlds – the emotional and rational – represented in the work. In the first production a simple costume change, into baggy trousers with the adoption of a white mask, distinguished the wicked cousin from the tender heroine. In the later productions, Shen-Te underwent a total physical metamorphosis when assuming the 'Mr Hyde' persona.

Melchinger describes the set on which the first production was staged:

Strehler and Damiani created their own version of Sichuan. Grey, hand-built huts with roofs made from white canvas framed in the surrounding cement, but as it were harmonised to the point of blending in with the pervading whiteness; and how well the white matches the grey! In one scene washing has been hung out to dry by the side of a hut; Brecht had always envisaged such a scene but the choice of *white* sheets blending in so perfectly – that was a Milanese touch.[21]

This stark, simple beauty of the setting with its genuinely original features was matched in the presentation of the three gods. Strehler did not overemphasise the satire (in the later productions they too were subjected to extreme directorial elaboration) but, rather, invested the comedy with human touches. When the third god says that he would prefer a house without spiders, for instance, he came downstage to tell the audience this and thus almost missed the flying machine which was transporting the others into the sky. At another point the three, weary of their attempt to find a good person, were seen sitting exhausted on their cases, 'a sculptured group which took on the force of a powerful image'. At the end, when they climb on to their pink cloud machine (one of the few touches of colour in the show), 'they only undertake the flight into the sky when they have securely closed themselves in, and they vanish, singing together, as the lights come up'.

Melchinger also describes Strehler's rehearsal technique. Employing musical terms, requesting a performer 'to deliver the lines a tone higher' he requires the poetic quality of the lines – the 'melody' – to emerge more clearly. At times the performer comes downstage and addresses the audience directly from the footlights. At these moments the actor is expressing the feelings of the audience:

According to Brecht's theory (which he was continuously revising, as his later writings reveal), the actor at such moments must step outside the role. With Strehler he transcends it. He doesn't allow the actor to diminish in any way the intensity of his identification with the role, rather he forces him to express a concentration of its emotional meaning.[22]

Melchinger adds: 'this is what I term "concentric theatre": intensity and form at the same moment'. Strehler is extremely meticulous, requiring the actor to convey every nuance of the personality and the situation. When this is not the case he calls for 'a moment's concentration' and waits in silence for two minutes. If the actor is still not delivering the full effect 'he jumps to his feet' and, Melchinger adds, 'his directorial genius manifests itself in a series of extraordinary inventions which no one would credit who had only wit-nessed the final results in the later performance':

He stalks up and down the stalls and throws himself into the delivery of a scene in the most intriguing manner. He becomes grandfather and little girl, boaster and barber, god and Shen-Te, mother and rebel. He doesn't just repeat Brecht's text but immerses himself in a sequence of outbursts in which the minutest point of significance becomes clear; he turns and addresses himself to imaginary people in the stalls, his eyes half closed, and states with absolute conviction things which are not so.[23]

When Strehler returned to *The Good Person of Setzuan* in 1977 he had a large number of Brecht stagings behind him and his political position had shifted; he had lost some of the optimism of the late fifties and was seeing issues in a harsher light. These factors strongly influenced the Hamburg production, which was at the same time more elaborate and more savage in its presentation of the world of Setzuan. The set – again by Damiani – was a revolving one, covered in pools of water and dominated by an image of the crater of a volcano glimpsed above the cyclorama; dustbins, used tyres, rubbish, the nose of an aeroplane with a broken propellor were scattered over it giving the impression of the suburbs of a third-world city.

The feature which both figuratively and thematically unifies this show is the water: the grey veil of fluid into which the people and the objects of Setzuan – Shen-Te's tent-cum-shop, Shui-Ta's van-cum-office – are sinking. We ought to remember that Strehler's *Lear*

14   Andrea Jonasson as Shen-Te in the Hamburg staging of *The Good Person of Setzuan*, 1977

was set in a similar territory: the visual metaphor for a desert or a prison. Precarious wooden beams traverse these little lakes of muddy water; they help to support the simple idyll of Shen-Te and the would-be pilot, Yang Suan (who turns into a cynical careerist). The water invades everything – the billing and cooing of the lovers, the girl's knees, the young man's side as he tries to stretch out next to her – giving rise to silent desperation, the awareness of the impossibility of being happy: we are sinking in the mire.[24]

In this setting the gods were presented in a far more critical, satirical light. On their first appearance, dressed in white and wearing dog-collars, they looked rather like Protestant ministers. Later they were seen in full evening dress in a box next to the stage, and subsequently they emerged from dustbins in a hilarious reference to Beckett and the theatre of the absurd.

The heroine had undergone a sea-change in the period separating the first and second productions:

The play is above all a testing ground for the actress. And Andrea Jonasson presents the two contrasted figures of Shen-Te and Shui-Ta as absolute opposites, showing remarkable theatrical skill in swapping from one to the other. She stresses the unaffected gentle humility of the former and endows the latter with a harsh robotic quality, a rigidity of movement and voice which creates the impression of a fierce marionette whose strings every so often snap under the pressure of emotion.[25]

When she repeated the role in Italy – and in Italian – the two aspects of the character seemed to have discovered new levels of meaning: she had enriched both the emotional appeal of the unworldly Shen-Te and developed the grotesqueness of Shui-Ta to a point of great intensity. The 'expressionist stylisation' of the Hamburg production which presented the wicked cousin as 'an operatic Chinese mandarin suffering from stomach ache' – as one critic (*Süddeutsche Zeitung*, 27 September 1977) described the impersonation) – developed into something more sinister. The critic of *L'Unità*, Aggeo Savioli, drew attention to the added sharpness of the characterisation and the increased political relevance of the show as a whole:

Brecht's message still has a meaning outside the historical circumstances which gave the play its birth; valid interpretation is still possible. Via the work's central imagery, Strehler meaningfully alludes to the past, the present and the future which this 'parable' contains or reflects. Thus the image of the ordinary factory takes on the overtones of a concentration camp with the ex-pilot in charge of it like a 'Kapo'. And we have Shui-Ta dressed entirely in black with black gloves, black bowler, dark glasses and shiny false teeth; employing a stiff walk, arms raised threateningly – something between Murnau's Nosferatu and Frankenstein's monster – a stylisation which inevitably conjures up both a boss and Hitler.[26]

He observed a richer dialectic in the show, drawing attention to the image of the water as having a positive significance. Whilst it is a source of great inconvenience and annoyance to the rich who try to avoid the puddles, it is a means of income for the water-seller, of diversion and pleasure to the poor (he recalls the significance of the puddle in Strehler's *Il campiello*), and it is under the rain that the lovers Shen-Te and Yang first meet. Strehler also extended the poetic and emotional force of the scene in which Shen-Te thinks of the future of her child in a dreamy reverie which never sank to the level of sentimentality.

In this third production the staging was simpler: there was still a revolve, but no vision of a volcano above the cyclorama, nor was the detritus strewn about the ground. Shen-Te's tobacco shop underwent another transformation. In the Hamburg version she had a makeshift construction, part tent, part broken-down van, which turned into a glistening illuminated vehicle when Shui-Ta took over. In the last production the shop was closer to those simple huts of the first staging, mobile (as a result of the revolve), though without their capacity for scuttling away when their inhabitants – at the beginning of the play – refused to help the gods. Strehler has continued to mine the potential of this work, discovering new areas of meaning and developing from a relatively simple staging through a highly elaborate one to a version which combined the merits of both. As de Monticelli has commented:

Strehler provides us with a scenic – not a literary – lesson in the greatness of Brecht's theatre; he teaches us to penetrate right to the heart of the various strata of meaning. To discover that below the most explicitly demonstrative and didactic level (the interplay of the masks between the characters of Shen-Te and Shui-Ta; the twin potential of the same person) there is a more touching and human level (the theme of Shen-Te's motherhood, for instance), and yet another which is profoundly ambiguous – and is mimed – in which the dramatist releases on us a sort of inspired clowning which serves to satirize social reality; what Roland Barthes has termed 'the partly arbitrary sign'.[27]

This third level – of inspired clowning – was at the centre of Strehler's next production of Brecht: *Schweyk in the Second World War*, a play totally different in style from either of the two he had staged previously. Brecht's adaptation of Jaroslav Hašek's satirical story required first and foremost an actor of immense comic force who was capable of handling the epic style. In discussing the play,

Strehler underlines its status as popular theatre which has a clear political purpose. The dramatic structure and the theatrical texture it gives rise to have one aim: to arouse in the mind of the audience a welter of ideological issues which can lead to a criticism – after the event – of the political system of the Nazis, as the show follows the adventures of an ordinary man who becomes involved by accident in the machinery of the system. This character, however – and it is vital to observe this – functions as a positive critical force even though his personality and behaviour are quite lacking in positive characteristics.[28]

From Schweyk's arrest at the end of the first scene, and throughout his interrogation, his second arrest, imprisonment and subsequent adventures, which lead to a confrontation with the Führer himself in the middle of the Russian steppes, we observe a character who, whilst he appears completely idiotic, behaves with a very individual logic of his own and thereby exposes the futility and madness of his oppressors. It is – Strehler argued – the basic unawareness of the character which must govern the actor's performance: 'Being calm, serene and unperturbable defines both the ethical and the epic features of this character who, though involved in a drama, doesn't have any dramas of his own.'[29] Strehler was fortunate in having Tino Buazzelli to play Schweyk. This huge (in every sense of the word) actor, a sort of cross between Oliver Hardy and Dario Fo, had taken over the role of Peachum when Strehler revised *The Threepenny Opera* in 1958 and had thus experienced the fusion of comedy and political satire basic to that play and production. As Schweyk he was required to play a very different character, a more genial figure of popular theatre whose innocent frankness makes him the victim of circumstances. Buazzelli employed his physical size and enormous, endlessly expressive face, to great effect:

a sort of broad, solid, compact serenity constantly radiates optimism which is given added vitality through the movements of that big agile body. He is neither the sort of person you take to right away, nor the reverse: he strikes a balance somewhere between the two.[30]

His vast range of facial and bodily expression springs out from the photographs of the production, particularly in the interrogation scene: the grotesquely exaggerated goose-step, the mockery of the bull-faced Nazi (when he temporarily appropriates Bullinger's hat and gun), the hunched position of devilish schoolboy glee. These endless chameleon-like shifts of appearance, accentuated by the bulk of his huge body, are all the more satirically effective for being overlooked throughout the scene by the picture of the po-faced Führer, and guaranteed to drive his interrogator to distraction.

Buazzelli has discussed the problems of interpreting the part, defining them as essentially falling into two categories: the choice of theatrical language and the potential remoteness of the figure for Italians. He points out that Brecht gave his Czech characters a Bohemian dialect to distinguish them from the Germans; since Schweyk is in turn set apart from his countrymen it is even more important that the actor discover a distinctive manner of speaking. He had at first considered employing a Roman accent but Strehler was unhappy with this and they decided on adopting a cadence and syntax which was recognisably proletarian, yet not coloured by any specific dialect. On the matter of relating the character and action to Italian conventions he discusses Schweyk as a 'mask', concluding:

It is no coincidence that I have talked about a mask. In my opinion Schweyk has one thing in common with our theatrical tradition: that is the commedia dell'arte. Isn't Pulcinella 'the small man who takes advantage of what small opportunities are left to him', as Brecht says of Schweyk? Isn't he a sort of Arlecchino, Brighella – those representatives and archetypes of our theatrical tradition? Schweyk is part of this great family, though he is in many ways very different, of course. And it was by beginning with these differences and similarities that Strehler and I explored and carefully considered the ways in which this great character can appeal to the tastes and conventions of an Italian audience, without thereby diminishing his significance.[31]

Brecht – who made his love of Italian commedia very clear to Strehler in their first conversations, and who is caught in a particularly affecting photograph taken during the rehearsals in Milan clutching his cap and the Arlecchino mask he had been given – would undoubtedly have appreciated this parallel.

The setting for Schweyk's actions was realised by Strehler and Damiani with considerable originality. The three different types of location – corresponding to the scenes in Prague, those in the 'Upper Spheres' (where Brecht parodies Goethe to present his vision of the Nazi leaders) and the final ones on the Russian steppes – presented particular challenges on the small stage of the Piccolo. The crucial central scenes which take place in the inn, the *Calice*, were the closest to the style of epic realism which had characterised Strehler's version of *The Threepenny Opera*, and were realised in a similar way. A raised area defined by five movable walls acted as a sort of 'Chinese box' resting just inside the confines of the stage; it was

a sort of Noah's ark – as Strehler came to define it – in which people come together during the flood, a fragile nutshell (the flats that constitute the walls are in fact thin and slightly warped) but one which won't sink. For this reason, the *Calice* is the only setting in which everything is tangible, solid, properly constructed, markedly realistic, with all the healthiness that real things possess, clearly made to last.[32]

A grey blackcloth fell rapidly to mark the beginning of the episode on the steppes. The only other scenic features employed here were a signpost, the hut belonging to the two women and a few pieces of furniture in the dream sequence of the *Calice*. At the height of the snowstorm the very realistic apparition of the tank with the soldiers intoning the Miserere was all the more powerful. By contrast projections were utilised elsewhere in the production along with a minimum of props. Strehler cut the map of the world, the model of the tank and the map of the Soviet Union requested by Brecht in the prologue and the intermezzi in the 'Upper Spheres', replacing them with features which emphasised more tellingly the political satire. The Nazi leaders were made much larger than life through the employment of stilts, their voices being projected through microphones and distorted so as to recall the way they had been relayed – via loudspeakers and over the radio – during the war.

This drama – which Strehler sees as part of a trilogy along with *Fear and Misery in the Third Reich* and *Arturu Ui* – is a particularly significant one for

the director and his generation. If he employed the production in some senses
to exorcise memories of the war, there is more to it than that, as Guazzotti has
pointed out:

Schweyk is a work of violent and studied denigration, conceived and employed in the face
of Nazism as a weapon to fight from the stage – just as Chaplin's The Great Dictator did
from the screen – the folly of a society prey to the most terrifying process of
degeneration. In fact the central theme of Schweyk – and for Strehler the poetic starting-
point – resides not so much in the invective and savage satire (dramatically significant
though they are) as in the analysis and awareness of the relationship between ordinary
people and the war, in the discovery of an irrepressible life-force which makes men turn
away from violence and look first of all to the escape-route of irony and from that to the
more positive and revolutionary solution of solidarity.[33]

Buazzelli was Strehler's Galileo in the most lauded of all his Brecht
stagings in 1963. The Italian press was unanimous in its praise of the
production which fused epic and realistic techniques and which had a rare
poetic richness combining – like his Lear a decade later – a limpid clarity with
an exhaustive exploration of the work's complex dialectic. The Times critic,
though not fully endorsing the Milanese opinion that it was 'the greatest
theatrical event since the war', drew attention to Damiani's design concept
which mirrored the achievement of the acting and direction:

As a spectacle the Piccolo's Teatro's Vita di Galileo is thrice-inspired. Brecht has left clear
instructions as to how the piece should be staged; and Mr Strehler, following these
instructions with all the genius of the great producer he is, has Luciano Damiani's decor to
help him give expression to his own interpretation of them. The basic set is the skeleton
of a stage such as Galileo's contemporary, Niccolo Sabbatini, might have used for the
display of his ingenious machines, though it is only the traverse curtains here that are
operated mechanically. This setting ensures, as Brecht intended, that the public is kept
constantly aware of the fact that they are in a theatre. The scenery itself consists of large
architectural drawings mounted on screens that are manipulated by soft-footed scene-
shifters. These suggest the locality and the period of the various episodes of the play
without in any way forming a naturalistic surrounding. The colours are subdued and
those of the costumes tone with the pen-and-wash effects of the background. Detail and
realism are reserved for the properties and furnishings of each scene.[34]

In his description of the rehearsals, Ferruccio Marotti discusses how Strehler
'whilst researching an in-depth psychological study of the characters
gradually obtained an epic analysis'. One scene illustrates the results very
clearly: that between Galileo and the little monk, Fulgenzio (Scene 8), in
which the actor must convey a complex series of motivations, simultaneously operating between a variety of Stanislavskian intentions and
objectives whilst at the same time alienating the character and situation,
forcing us to appreciate their complexity. We must be aware of the young
friar's sincerity, his goodness, his shyness and his effort in talking to Galileo,
yet we must appreciate too that a subconscious objective is to be proved

wrong so that he can take up the research the church forbids him to pursue. The friar's physical gestures and way of speaking must reflect his training: the tendency to underline things with a gesture before he speaks; a trick of enunciating the words a little too carefully so as to give a faint impression of delivering a sermon. Renato de Carmine gave powerful theatrical expression to Strehler's concept:

The director has subtly resolved this issue via the most gentle, carefully modulated, one could say musical delivery of the lines; the setting is wholly abstract, outside reality; a stage which is bare except for the bench Galileo is sitting on, bathed in the clearest light, pure as the young friar's soul. The gestures which accompany Fulgenzio's pleading are slow, laboured, carefully enunciated, yet at the same time timid and hesitant. The observer understands every aspect of his problem, comprehends every detail of his behaviour, but at the same time disapproves of what he is saying because he is resorting to concepts of spiritual and everyday life which are non-existent and is ignoring the historical perspective. In this way a dialectic of feeling versus reason is set up in which the latter wins through yet leaves room for Pascal's 'reasons of the heart'.[35]

In each scene Strehler crystallised the complexity of the issues, intensifying the play's poetic force with inventions of his own. In the scene where Galileo encounters the two cardinals and is persuaded to abandon the Copernican theory (Scene 7) he was dressed in a rich baroque cloak so as to resemble the God of the Tiber. His appearance was made to contrast markedly with the

15   Damiani's set for the first scene of *Galileo*, 1963 (Tino Buazzelli as Galileo)

sombre aspect of the cardinals: one enters from behind the wing downstage left and the other from behind the one upstage right; they carry fans which they open and snap closed as they exchange biblical quotations, hovering round him so as to trap him continuously at the centre of the diagonal they maintain throughout the confrontation. When they take him off, defeated, the rhythm of the dancers who from time to time emerge from the background and cross the stage changes to that of a funeral dirge. At the end of the scene with the scholars (Scene 9), when he is persuaded to take up his research again, the stage darkens and a blazing sun is seen at the centre of the backcloth. As the students advance, 'like shadows searching for the truth in the dark', Fulgenzio makes a gesture of adoration. There is a pause and the gloom is lit up by the whiteness of Virginia's wedding-dress as she enters looking for Lodovico. Recognising that he has left, she stops in her tracks, petrified, accuses her father of sending him away and falls down in a swoon. The scene in which Galileo renounces his beliefs (Scene 13) had several powerful directorial innovations. When the bells do not sound at first, Fulgenzio, believing Galileo has not abjured, falls to his knees intoning the Gloria, whilst Virginia on the other side of the stage, bent over in grief, murmurs the Miserere. When the bells do sound, Fulgenzio, as if he has been mortally wounded, begins to chant the Miserere, whilst Virginia, arms raised to heaven, bursts into the Gloria now her father is saved from damnation. When Galileo then enters, dragging his way across the room, he is virtually unrecognisable. The sight is terrifying: he has visibly aged and his face is deathly white; one hand is curled up in revulsion at the memory of the instruments of torture he has been shown. 'Then he turns suddenly to the audience with a fiendish grin, that of a child, of someone who has narrowly escaped death, but at too high a price.'[36]

There follows a blackout as he sits on the bench; in the darkness a roll of drums is heard and the town crier reads out the abjuration. When the lights come up Virginia has gone and Andrea is left to shout his curse: 'Unhappy the land that has no more heroes!' The disciples split up, go their different ways. Galileo retorts, exhausted: 'No, Andrea. Unhappy the land that still needs heroes!' and as the lights gradually dim to blackout the sound of drumrolls and the voices of the town criers echo into the distance Galileo's name and the words of his renunciation. This moment encapsulates Strehler's imaginative skills in realising the full richness of Brecht's theatre: simultaneously epic, human, gestic, poetic and musical. The keynote of the production was one of lyrical clarity, at its most sustained in the scene of the Pope's investiture:

Especially effective is the discussion between Urban VIII and the Cardinal Inquisitor in which, against a background of a sectional drawing of the cupola of Saint Peter's, the pope is ceremoniously enrobed. In this the formal washing of hands, the fussy little tinkle of the handbells and ominous boom of their big brother, all contribute without any over-emphasis to the significance of a dialogue that begins with the Pope's emphatic negative to what the Inquisitor has been asking, and ends with the reluctant consent of His Holiness, resplendent in spotless white, to Galileo's being confronted with the inquisitorial instruments of torture.[37]

At the end of the first run of *Galileo*, after fifty-six sold-out performances at the Piccolo and with the prospect of reviving the show later in the year before touring it, Strehler sent what is now a celebrated open letter to the actors in which he makes some important remarks on the problems of performing such a demanding work over a long period of time, comments which go to the heart of the challenge represented by epic theatre:

Always remember that if the danger of realistic theatre lies in its limitation, its tendency to narrow the perspective, to involve the audience psychologically and to work too exclusively on the emotions, the danger of epic theatre is a tendency to greyness, to an indulgently slow rhythm, to a mere syntactical precision of pronunciation (but – dear friends – never underestimate the importance of speaking the lines with the correct verbal and grammatical emphasis), to a lack of weight and texture . . . remember that narrative theatre is above all a *way of thinking*, a form of commitment. It teaches moral responsibility, choice. During any performance it may be that you experience difficulty in listening attentively to the other actors, you don't feel in the right mood, your performances seem stale; but it mustn't be possible whilst you're acting to abandon – even for a moment – your status as thinking creatures who exist because they think. Narrative theatre leaves you no escape-route: you know this – it requires at all times thought, attention, awareness. If these are lacking, it simply doesn't exist: there is a vacuum.[38]

Strehler's production of *St Joan of the Stockyards* (1970) was at the furthest extreme from his *Galileo* staging. It was undertaken in that period of his exile from the Piccolo; it was first mounted in Florence at the Teatro della Pergola during the Maggio Musicale and subsequently in Milan at the Lirico. It came between his production of Weiss's *Song of the Lusitanian Bogey* and his second version of *The Lower Depths*, and shared the intensity of political activism which marked those two shows. His concern was with the proletariat, the masses who are victims of capitalism: the crowd became the central character of the production, as he employed a group of over sixty to present this complex and contradictory protagonist. The need to stage this particular work and at that particular time was explained with an urgency and a sense of outrage:

Brecht in *Saint Joan of the Stockyards* demystifies the nobility of the system; he goes so far as to make the bosses speak in verse just like kings on the Elizabethan stage and has them discuss things which are made to appear noble but are quite the reverse: weeping because a white bull is to be massacred, for instance, or discussing the Chicago slaughterhouse in lyrical terms. At a time when there is a boom in consumer society it is difficult to see beyond the fine speaking, elegant clothes and social rituals so as to identify clearly the appalling and inescapable reality of this system and make a critique of society. Today we should be considering the problem not in terms of the Chicago slaughterhouses, the economic depression which led to the rise of Nazism, or the crisis in America but in a different context – we should be aware, rather, of the necessity to demystify the car, the hot-water supply and the television set. The issue we're faced with concerns these basic facts of consumerist life. It seems to me imperative that from a historical point of view we reveal that the monsters are right here amongst us.[39]

The production did not enjoy the unanimous approval of the critics, some of whom objected to the style of the show: conceived not in terms of poor theatre but on a more operatic level, with a multi-media emphasis drawing on cinematic techniques, musical effects and employing a rich vein of theatrical parody. The chorus was handled with the attention and refinement which was to characterise his staging of *Simon Boccanegra*. In the first scene – after the prologue with Mauler and Cridle – this vast group was seen in front of the railings of a factory which, with its barbed-wire fence and its black chimneys, gave the impression of a concentration camp. Their first utterance, 'Noi' ('We'), was punched straight at the audience and Strehler went on to orchestrate the whole of this opening speech giving it the force of a chorus from Greek tragedy, whilst counterpointing the emotional pleas of the crowd with the introductory sounds of the factory: escaping steam,

16   The opening scene of *St Joan of the Stockyards*, 1970

machinery and sirens. The idea for the appearance of the factory – which dominated the whole production – came from a volume of photographs by Bill Brandt entitled *Shadows of Light*. One picture in particular inspired Ezio Frigerio's design, which embodied and complemented the political concept central to Strehler's approach:

The image reeked of decay and prison: the chimneys were like towers: the smoke that came out of them seem pestilential (as though emerging from the chimneys of a concentration camp), a horrific smog. Everything was back-lit so that the factory had a sinister appearance.[40]

The production boasted a barrage of effects in accordance with Strehler's belief that political theatre has to be both entertaining and aesthetically appealing. The capitalists – from the champions of industry through to the men in the stock exchange – were presented in terms of parody. Slift was seen as a Mephisthophelean figure (particularly in his revelation to Joan of the evil of the poor in Scene 4) and Mauler had the stature of Richard III in his elimination of industrial competitors and his attempt to woo Joan to his ethic. In the stock exchange the chorus of stockbrokers entered goose-stepping and, after two parts of a funeral bier had been assembled to make a boxing ring, the confrontations between the rival leaders were acted out on it. References to silent cinema abounded:

Apart from the circus and music hall the director draws heavily on the silent cinema. The costumes are typical of the films of Chaplin: dress-suit, top-hat, white scarf and cane for the rich, their faces whitened like clowns, glowing under the stage lamps as they climb onto barbers' chairs familiar from *The Great Dictator* and from gangster movies; gags with custard pies are also Chaplinesque, as is the figure of the terrified little girl Joan becomes before she dies as a saint against her will – a powerful finale revealing how she had been manipulated by the bosses.[41]

Cinema also features in another more innovatory sense in the show. In order to present the conduct of the workers in such a way as to destroy Joan's faith in them, Slift showed her a film:

Strehler emphasises the importance of the film as the turning-point in Joan's story. It symbolises a descent into the Inferno via a carefully graded ladder. The film is discussed: it must be crudely made, the boss's documentary on the errors and wickedness of the workers. Strehler examines how this functions and what the motivations are. The film is to be an exercise in spying on the workers. The whole sequence is a lesson in epic theatre because everything is narrated and then shown. He has the idea that the different film extracts have been put together by an amateur working for the boss, who gets a kick out of spying on the workers and recording their behaviour.[42]

The scene in question opened with Slift sitting Joan forcefully on a canvas-backed film-director's seat which he opened up whilst an eight-foot-square screen descended half-way down the stage. The first piece of film showed a young worker being asked to dispose of the suit of a fellow employee who had been killed when he fell into a large vat. Slift himself was then seen on the film – spying on the boy, who has gone into the lavatory to change into the suit. Slift's pose – leaning nonchalantly, arms folded, observing the action with a sardonic smile – was precisely repeated on stage. The boy's cynical dismissal of the dead man caused Joan to bend over convulsed with pain; but Slift, stamping noisily on the floor, forced her to go on watching. A lengthy sequence counterpointing the stage action with that on screen culminated in Joan standing to address the audience directly with: 'You have shown me the abject condition of the poor; now I will show you their pain!'

The film was a brilliant innovation: the projection was cleverly faked in

17   The cinematic sequence in *St Joan of the Stockyards* (Valentina Cortese as Joan, Gigi Pistilli as Slift and Cesarina Gheraldi (on screen) as Mrs Luckerniddle)

performance with the reel appearing to run out, break down or – at one point – catch fire. Based on naturalistic criteria of how and why it had been made, it was an outstanding example of Strehler's originality in employing the techniques of epic drama.

For Strehler, Brecht is undoubtedly the most important of all theatrical artists. This is reflected in the productions of his work: five plays, two *Lehrstücke*, two music theatre pieces and a series of anthologies. But it is even more evident in the influence of his theory and practice on Strehler's stagings of work by other dramatists. Techniques of epic theatre were clearly in evidence in his versions of *Coriolanus* and *Il gioco dei potenti*, whilst the rich dialectic of *King Lear* was realised with remarkable force. The social perspective of Brecht's theatre found a strong echo in the two mature Goldoni productions: *Le baruffe chiozzotte* and *Il campiello*. Again we come face to face with that trio of dramatists most close to Strehler: Goldoni, Shakespeare, Brecht. And whilst there are complex themes and dramatic features subtly uniting the three, it is Brecht who most fully characterises and defines the network of interrelated motifs which bind them inexorably together in the Strehler canon.

6   Lyric opera

What is really needed is a proper musical education for a new public; instead of that phoney Italian passion for opera: an elitist ideal based on snobbery and ignorance. I'm talking about a broader understanding of music and opera in which voice, acting, stage presence, style, singing, orchestral playing and staging are equally important and seen as complementary – not as mere exhibitions of showmanship on the part of conductors or performers. Opera must move in this direction. It should be possible, after all, to run excellent companies with few divas – preferably none at all. And the public needs to be taught this.

Strehler, 'Operaddio!', Teatro in Europa 2 (1987), p. 59

Music is fundamental to Strehler's theatre. When we remember that Strehler chose to launch his career as a director of Brecht with *The Threepenny Opera* (and that two other Brecht pieces he has undertaken, *Mahagonny* and *Lucullus*, are essentially pioneer works of modern music theatre); when we look at the long list of his opera stagings, at La Scala and abroad; when we consider the lyrical features of so many of his productions, from Chekhov through to Bertolazzi; and when we observe that the play which Strehler regards as a theatrical touchstone – *The Tempest* – is a drama in which music and its power play an important part, we appreciate what is the most original and significant aspect of his skill as a director.

In examining music and its importance for Strehler we are able not so much to sum up his achievement as to comprehend the parameters of his theatrical genius. Strehler inherited his musical skills from his mother, a distinguished violinist. We have already alluded to the comment of Victor de Sabata during the *Pelléas and Mélisande* production at La Scala in 1949 – a comment to which Strehler still refers. In a recent interview in the magazine *Teatro in Europa* he tells us why he did not take up a career as an orchestral conductor: 'I chose – and I confess this with a feeling of painful sacrifice – the Piccolo and straight theatre. I chose the hard road: that of reforming the Italian theatre.'

His comment touches on a wide number of issues: the whole Italian tradition of theatre – 'teatro di prosa' as against 'teatro lirico'; the issue of reform – of educating the Italian public to appreciate a new repertoire, one which would place Italian drama in a wider European context; the formation of a resident, permanent company to combat the outmoded conventions of touring and the tyranny of the leading actor; the consequent need for collaboration – for working with a dedicated group of friends, allies, kindred

117

spirits – to fight prejudice and ignorance; the need, above all else, to provide a public service: to create a need, fulfil it and, in so doing, create a *teatro umano*.

Looking at each of these issues in the light of Strehler's career in the opera house illuminates his overall achievement, placing it in a more meaningful context. Glancing through the list of Strehler's opera productions, one is struck by the versatility of his skills and the rate at which he was working in the earlier years. In 1949 he undertook productions of Cimarosa, Debussy, Petrassi and Berg; whilst in one month – May 1950 – he staged pieces as different as Malipiero's *L'allegra brigata*, Donizetti's *Don Pasquale* and Strauss's *Ariadne auf Naxos* – all at La Scala. This is entirely characteristic of the pace of his work in the straight theatre at this time; but it should be realised that an opera production – in the foremost Italian (if not world) house – signifies something more. It represents a challenge and – in Strehler's case – an achievement on an altogether larger scale. It is the challenge which only a multi-media piece can offer. The risk of failure – of the delicate balance between acting and singing, between musical director and stage director, being lost – is great. When all the elements come together – as they did most triumphantly in the *Pelléas and Mélisande* production – there is a sense of achievement which, in Strehler's case, gave way to a dilemma as to which path to pursue.

Though Strehler chose not to take up the conductor's baton, in a sense he has wielded one ever since. To watch him rehearse is rather like watching an orchestral conductor at work. In *L'Illusion*, for instance, which he remounted in Milan with the French cast shortly after its Paris premiere, he constantly punctuated their delivery with precise vocal instructions (in French): 'project', 'deeper', 'louder', 'more emphasis', 'hold on to that', and so on, whilst at the same time issuing complex orders to the technicians (in Italian). In the *Teatro in Europa* interview he draws attention to the monumental problems involved in staging *Don Giovanni* at La Scala now. Things have changed radically in the last forty years: we are into the age of the opera star as international commuter, a factor which serves to perpetuate the bad old conventions of the nineteenth-century stage which Strehler had combated in the 1940s. La Scala is Italy's leading opera house and it thrives on stars who with their international careers have little time for rehearsal and little inclination to rethink a role in the light of a fresh production. They are the contemporary *mattatori*, taking the theatre back to that stage in the immediate post-war period when the prompt box was still a crucial feature (it was some time before Strehler persuaded his earlier actors to do without it) and when the performers were suspicious of playing at the same venue for fear of over-familiarisation. Modern opera stars such as Pavarotti, Domingo or Caballé can repeat their Otellos, Nemorinos and Normas all over the world to the delight of different audiences; to stay in one place with one company for any length of time is an altogether different test.

Any final assessment of Strehler's achievement or definition of his style of theatre begins and ends with a discussion of the repertoire. This is equally the case with opera. The list of composers Strehler has ignored tells us a great deal. He has never directed any work by Rossini, Bellini, Puccini or Berio. As against four Verdi stagings he has undertaken only one of a Wagner opera: of *Lohengrin* in 1981. The issue of Wagner's fortunes in Italy, tied up as they are with his reputation during the war as a result of Hitler's relationship with Bayreuth, is complex. Bologna took up the Wagner challenge in his lifetime and continues to champion his work. It is easy to see why Strehler is more drawn – as was Grassi – to Verdi, though one cannot help regretting that he has never tackled *The Ring*. He doubtless feels that Wagner is best left in other hands: those of his protegé Patrice Chéreau, for example, whose 1976 Bayreuth *Ring* carried Strehlerian revaluation to a masterful height.

Rossini's epicurean style does not accord with Strehler's ethic (Ronconi has scored some of his more remarkable successes by imposing stunningly imaginative scenic effects on *Il viaggio a Reims* and *William Tell*: the antithesis of Strehler's method). Neither Puccini's politics nor his over-emotional statement of issues accord with Strehler's approach. His avoidance of the Bellini canon is explained by the fact that Visconti (with Callas) scored a particular success with his operas in the fifties at La Scala and left little room for that revaluation which is at the heart of Strehler's fascination with theatre. His interest in twentieth-century music theatre has not extended to Berio (or Nono), though the pioneers of this movement – Stravinsky, Brecht (with Weill and Eisler) and Berg – have featured significantly throughout Strehler's career. *The Soldier's Tale* has remained a constant source of reference. The need to discover a fresh theatrical language through which to express this original amalgamation of music and drama – a concept of theatre quite different from (and often opposed to) opera – complements Strehler's researches into areas of straight theatre.

In looking through the catalogue of musical works he has staged we are struck by their affinity with Strehler's tastes in straight theatre. There is a frequent return to works which relate to the conventions of commedia: from Cimarosa and Donizetti (significantly Strehler has not touched his more celebrated tragic operas, *Lucia di Lammermoor* or *Maria Stuarda*, for instance) through to *Ariadne auf Naxos* and *The Love of Three Oranges*. Given his professed dislike for Gozzi, his frequent return to the Prokofiev (based on the very play which sparked off the rivalry with Goldoni) is fascinating. On the other hand he has been drawn consistently to works in the verismo repertoire, from *Cavalleria rusticana* through to Charpentier's *Louise*, the natural complement to his lyrical stagings of realistic prose pieces. It is interesting to observe that he has not directed the opera closely linked to *Cavalleria rusticana*, *I pagliacci*, despite its verismo pretensions and employment of commedia conventions. It is a mark of his taste that he sees through this cardboard work, preferring – in a genre which exploits the play-within-the-play – to direct Malipiero's *La favola del figlio cambiato*, the companion piece to (and play performed by the company in) *The Mountain Giants*.

The combination of Strehler's theatrical interests and skills is most evident in his staging of Mozart. The fusion of Italian and Teutonic temperament is common to both composer and director, whilst the humanity of the operas expressed through an unparalleled musical precision makes them for Strehler the ultimate challenge. And it is in this context that Strehler has experienced some of his greatest frustrations. Take the *Don Giovanni*, his latest essay in Mozart, which was in some real senses a failure; or, more precisely, a compromise. In an international opera house (even, in this case, La Scala) Strehler is not in control of the casting, and it is here that his longing for a genuinely European, international theatre is put to the test. Opera is by its very nature the most international of theatrical forms. Artists of different nationalities perform together; they are often fluent (as straight actors are not) in several languages; the audience readily accepts the fact that the work is being performed in a foreign language (and has gone to some lengths to prepare itself for the experience). Perversely, the international language of opera is Italian; for historical and cultural reasons Italian is international in no other sense; and this is confusing in Strehler's search for a European theatre.

Strehler directed *Don Giovanni* for the opening of the 1987 La Scala season on 7 December, the feast of Milan's patron saint, Ambrose, and the most prestigious date in the Italian artistic calendar (tickets are sold for astronomical prices). He let it be known that though he had no objection to the cultural event being televised, he did not wish the production itself to be recorded. The statement was perhaps ingenuous, but it was complicated by the fact that the staging, which emphasised the nocturnal aspect of the work, was notoriously difficult to record. Financial interests overrode his idealism and he was forced to accept not only that three out of the eleven performances were filmed with extra lighting (which totally destroyed the stage picture for the theatre-goers) but that during the run roles were taken by different singers from those with whom he had rehearsed. By the last performance only Claudio Desderi, the Leporello, remained from the original cast.

In the *Teatro in Europa* article he laments these compromises and expresses the opinion that under these circumstances the limitations of opera staging outstrip the challenges. Two years later he walked out just before the Paris premiere of his *Fidelio* because the soprano was replaced at the last minute. This is frustrating for someone who has worked for months with cast, orchestra, designer and technicians. But it is the world of opera. It will be interesting to see whether his ideal of a European theatrical community manages to evade these problems. There are other – immediately practical – solutions to the problem of operatic staging in this context. Ronconi, for instance, has triumphed by emphasising the static monumental aspects of grand opera and by moving his actor-singers (rather as Edward Gordon Craig intended) like marionettes; his La Scala *Ernani* and *Lodoïska* are examples of this.

Nor is Strehler prepared – like Peter Stein – to take up the challenge of working with a company such as Welsh National Opera. He has applauded Stein's courage, but it is clear that he finds the enterprise provincial; he feels (rightly or wrongly) that he would be compromising his musical standards to work in this way. And after forty years at La Scala this is not an unreasonable assumption. However, the sort of operatic theatre he wants – one without stars and with a total integration of musical and dramatic skills – was achieved at the Komische Oper in East Berlin by Felsenstein and is very much a part of the policy of a company like Welsh National. Whether you can have all this and the finest singers in the world remains the problem.

Strehler's other experiences in directing Mozart are equally revealing. In 1973 he staged *The Marriage of Figaro* at the Paris Opera. He rehearsed for several weeks and then the conductor, Solti, came in to take over – which is precisely what he did. He altered the director's tempi (even though Strehler had been working from the conductor's own metronome markings) and made it clear that his services were not required at this stage of rehearsal. If Strehler was embittered by this, he was saddened by his attempt to work with Karajan on *The Magic Flute* at Salzburg in 1974. He realised that whilst Karajan was that rare phenomenon – the orchestral conductor with a flair for direction – his theatrical insights into the work were traditional, banal even, and that here was no room for collaboration.

The experiences with Solti and Karajan came between his two most triumphant opera stagings: of *Simon Boccanegra* and *Macbeth* at La Scala. When opera works – when there is a complete fusion of musical, dramatic and theatrical skills – it produces an effect like no other theatrical medium. This is the ideal to which Strehler, the perfectionist, aspires. The same is true of the Théâtre de l'Europe: it is a dream, not a chimera. The reason for the success of the two Verdi productions explains Strehler's skill in both the prose and the lyric theatre. It is dependent upon a level of collaboration between all the artists involved. These productions marked the height of Strehler's work with Grassi; in both cases the conductor was Abbado; the designer of *Boccanegra* was Frigerio, of *Macbeth* Damiani, the two artists who have given scenic expression to Strehler's ideas throughout his later career. Moreover, Strehler was working with a company of singers under ideal rehearsal conditions.

It is this type of collaboration which has also made the Piccolo the focus of Italian theatrical culture and which Strehler valiantly seeks to extend into a wider European context. It is an undertaking actors were wary of when Strehler set up the Piccolo company and it is a major achievement to have educated both performers and public to appreciate a different set of values. This is the secret of Strehler's theatrical revolution. What effect it has had outside Milan is another matter. Take Gabriele Lavia, for instance: Strehler's Edgar, an actor of remarkable force. He now runs his own company in the best nineteenth-century tradition (his wife, Monica Guerritore, is his leading lady), directing and starring in plays which are performed all over Italy. These plays are invariably classics: by Shakespeare, Schiller, Sophocles, Strindberg, carefully tailored to his own individual histrionic skills. But this type of theatre perpetuates a very outmoded critical attitude to the repertoire. And here is where Strehler's revaluation of the repertoire has to be seen in a different perspective. He has made Milan, then Italy and (to some extent) the rest of Europe, aware of the strengths of underrated or neglected plays and authors, and he has revealed fresh meaning and relevance in better-known works. But what does this achievement count for in a theatre governed by considerations of box-office and influenced by British theatrical agents who will promote Frayn and Ayckbourn rather than Pinter or Bond?

Strehler, it must be admitted, has no more changed the tastes of the average theatre-goer (or management) in Italy than he has changed the nature and composition of the companies. The fact that there is no other *teatro stabile* with the same sort of integrity as the Piccolo underlines his determination and courage. But it is depressing to look through the list of plays performed in Italy: a diet of contemporary British and American bourgeois comedies with the odd Italian classic (usually Pirandello or Betti). Not only Brecht stopped at Milan. And in some respects Strehler must take the responsibility.

Born in that most cosmopolitan of cities, Trieste, of middle-European parentage, his cultural horizons were from the start broad. His love of French theatre and his debt to his two 'maestri', Copeau and Jouvet, sealed his commitment to foreign theatre. But, like many Italian intellectuals of his generation, this culture excludes Britain. With the exception of *Murder in the Cathedral* Strehler has never undertaken a production of a play by a British dramatist other than Shakespeare. This comes as quite a shock – perhaps a salutary one, given the complacent British assumption as to the strengths of its dramatic tradition. In the field of modern theatre this is a noticeable gap in Strehler's culture. There is little likelihood of his being drawn to Beckett-influenced writers such as Stoppard or Pinter or of his wishing to be involved with the polemics of Arden and D'Arcy, Edgar or Brenton, which must appear to him provincial and lacking in true dialectic. But his refusal to take on Bond is more revealing. Critics and friends tried to interest him in staging Bond's *Lear* (which was premiered in Britain shortly before his own production of the Shakespeare), but he declined, finding the piece crude and unpoetic. That it is neither tells us more about the lack of an adequate translation (given Strehler's inability to speak or read English) rather than insensitivity on his part. But it is regrettable that a play so in tune with Strehler's ethical and theatrical preoccupations, by a writer who shares his views on the import-ance of rational and humane values above all else, should have been neglected.

Nevertheless, Strehler's achievement – to reanimate Italian traditions within the context of the European repertoire – should not be underesti-mated. The reason why his Brecht productions have been so successful is that he has related the epic features of the plays to recognisable Italian models, from the cabaret and variety routines employed in *The Threepenny Opera* to the operatic style chosen for *St Joan of the Stockyards*. It is Italianate lyricism and comic improvisation which have given many of his Shakespeare productions their particular character and force.

And Strehler has quietly brought about a revolution in acting. He has refined basic aspects of the Italian tradition – as different as comic improvisation and the powerfully gestic emphasis particular to opera – through the ethical teaching of Copeau and Jouvet, the naturalistic example of Stanislavski and the rigorous practice of Brecht's epic theatre. Audiences and critics remember him for encouraging performances of extraordinary bravura and versatility – from Valentina Cortese's Liuba through to Andrea Jonasson's Shui-Ta/Shen-Te, and more recently Gérard Desarthe's brilliant doubling of Alcandre and Matamore. Versatility is a hallmark of the Strehler style. But the greatest monuments to his skills as a director are those shows in which, after months – even years – of research and rehearsal the contrasted features of the works have stood out in the clearest relief, stripped of any irrelevant or distracting feature. It is the productions of *King Lear, Galileo, The Tempest* (in the second version) and the final 'farewell' *Arlecchino* which in the naked simplicity of their staging have revealed these dramas in their full depth and complexity.

Chronology

This is a complete list of all Strehler's productions to date. If a work appears more than once this implies a new staging. I have kept the titles of operas in the original language if they are better known by these names.

Date	Playwright	Title	Theatre
1943			
24 Jan.	Pirandello	*Triple bill*	Teatro di Casa Littoria, Novara
8 May	Gaudioso	*A Heaven*	Teatro di Casa Littoria, Novara
	Joppolo	*The Walk*	Teatro di Casa Littoria, Novara
1943–4			
	Pirandello	*Triple bill*	POW camp, Murren
1945			
14 April	Eliot	*Murder in the Cathedral*	Théâtre de la Comédie, Geneva
27 June	Camus	*Caligula*	Théâtre de la Comédie, Geneva
July	Wilder	*Our Town*	Théâtre de la Comédie, Geneva
15 Dec.	O'Neill	*Mourning Becomes Electra*	Teatro Odeon, Milan
1946			
5 Jan.	Camus	*Caligula*	Teatro della Pergola, Florence
19 March	Honegger	*Joan of Arc at the Stake*	Teatro alla Scala, Milan
4 June	Zola	*Thérèse Raquin*	Teatro Odeon, Milan
15 June	O'Neill	*Desire under the Elms*	Teatro Odeon, Milan
27 June	Salacrou	*A Free Woman*	Teatro Odeon, Milan
11 July	Anderson	*Winterset*	Teatro Odeon, Milan
9 Nov.	Flaiano	*War Explained to the Poor*	Teatro Excelsior, Milan
16 Nov.	Buzzati	*The Revolt against the Poor*	Teatro Excelsior, Milan
26 Nov.	Gorky	*The Petite Bourgeoisie*	Teatro Excelsior, Milan
17 Dec.	Shelley	*Pick-up Girl*	Teatro Nuovo, Milan
1947			
6 March	Verdi	*La traviata*	Teatro alla Scala, Milan
7 March	Kaiser	*The Soldier Tanaka*	Teatro Olimpia, Milan
14 May	Gorky	*The Lower Depths*	Piccolo Teatro, Milan
6 June	Salacrou	*The Nights of Rage*	Piccolo Teatro, Milan
8 July	Calderón	*The Prodigious Magician*	Piccolo Teatro, Milan
24 July	Goldoni	*Arlecchino, the Servant of Two Masters*	Piccolo Teatro, Milan
16 Oct.	Pirandello	*The Mountain Giants*	Piccolo Teatro, Milan
11 Nov.	Ostrovsky	*The Storm*	Piccolo Teatro, Milan
30 Dec.	Prokofiev	*The Love of Three Oranges*	Teatro alla Scala, Milan
1948			
26 Feb.	Baty (Dostoyevsky)	*Crime and Punishment*	Piccolo Teatro, Milan

125

Date	Playwright	Title	Theatre
23 April	Shakespeare	Richard II	Piccolo Teatro, Milan
6 June	Shakespeare	The Tempest	Boboli Gardens, Florence
26 July	Shakespeare	Romeo and Juliet	Teatro Romano, Verona
21 Aug.	Eliot	Murder in the Cathedral	Church of San Francesco, San Miniato
26 Sept.	Gozzi	The Crow	Teatro La Fenice, Venice
24 Nov.	Chekov	The Seagull	Piccolo Teatro, Milan
29 Dec.	Wilder	The Skin of Our Teeth	Piccolo Teatro, Milan
1949			
11 Feb.	Shakespeare	The Taming of the Shrew	Piccolo Teatro, Milan
22 March	Cimarosa	Il matrimonio segreto	Teatro alla Scala, Milan
7 April	Debussy	Pelléas and Mélisande	Teatro alla Scala, Milan
11 May	Bontempelli	People in Their Time	Piccolo Teatro, Milan
12 May	Petrassi	Il cordovano	Teatro alla Scala, Milan
4 Sept.	Berg	Lulu	Teatro La Fenice, Venice
1 Oct.	Pirandello	The Mountain Giants	Schauspielhaus, Zurich
24 Oct.	Pirandello	Tonight We Improvise	Teatre des Champs Elysées, Paris
20 Dec.	Ibsen	Little Eyolf	Piccolo Teatro, Milan
1950			
18 Jan.	Becque	The Women of Paris	Piccolo Teatro, Milan
15 Feb.	Shakespeare	Richard III	Piccolo Teatro, Milan
11 March	Molière	Don Juan	Schauspielhaus, Zurich
3 May	Camus	The Just	Piccolo Teatro, Milan
4 May	Malipiero	L'allegra brigata	Teatro alla Scala, Milan
20 May	Donizetti	Don Pasquale	Teatro alla Scala, Milan
27 May	Strauss	Ariadne auf Naxos	Teatro alla Scala, Milan
1 June	Savinio	Alcestis	Piccolo Teatro, Milan
15 June	Perosi	Il Nazzareno	Teatro alla Scala, Milan
20 July	Goldoni	The Good Girl	Campo San Trovaso, Venice
8 Sept.	Trissino	Sophonisba	Teatro Olimpico, Vicenza
8 Oct.	Goldoni	The Lovers	Teatro Sociale, Lecco
17 Oct.	Williams	Summer and Smoke	Piccolo Teatro, Milan
16 Nov.	Molière	The Misanthropist	Teatro Sociale, Lecco
15 Dec.	Büchner	Danton's Death	Teatro Sociale, Lecco
1951			
14 Feb.	Ibsen	A Doll's House	Piccolo Teatro, Milan
24 Feb.	Piccinni	La Checchina o la buona figliuola	Teatro alla Scala, Milan
9 March	Donizetti	L'elisir d'amore	Teatro alla Scala, Milan
21 March	Giovaninetti	Fool's Gold	Piccolo Teatro, Milan
18 April	Massenet	Werther	Teatro alla Scala, Milan
20 April	De Musset	Never Swear by Anything	Piccolo Teatro, Milan
11 May	Betti	Disaster at the North Depot	Piccolo Teatro, Milan
12 May	Peragallo	La collina	Teatro alla Scala, Milan
4 June	Molière	Don Juan	Freie Volksbühne, Berlin
14 June	Honegger	Judith	Teatro alla Scala, Milan
7 July	Shakespeare	Henry IV	Teatro Romano, Verona
25 Aug.	Shakespeare	Twelfth Night	Palazzo Grassi, Venice
7 Sept.	Sophocles	Electra	Teatro Olimpico, Vicenza
27 Oct.	(double bill) Goldoni	The Army Lover	Piccolo Teatro, Milan
	Molière	The Flying Doctor	Piccolo Teatro, Milan

Date	Playwright	Title	Theatre
20 Nov.	Toller	*Hoppla, Such Is Life*	Piccolo Teatro, Milan
26 Dec.	Cimarosa	*Il credulo*	Teatro alla Scala, Milan
1952			
31 Jan.	Shakespeare	*Macbeth*	Piccolo Teatro, Milan
27 Feb.	Zardi	*Emma*	Piccolo Teatro, Milan
17 March	Castro	*Proserpina and the Stranger*	Teatro alla Scala, Milan
17 April	Goldoni	*Arlecchino, the Servant of Two Masters*	Teatro Quirino, Rome
16 May	Vergani	*Walking on Water*	Piccolo Teatro, Milan
10 Sept.	Malipiero	*La favola del figlio cambiato*	Teatro La Fenice, Venice
22 Nov.	Bruckner	*Elizabeth of England*	Piccolo Teatro, Milan
11 Dec.	Gogol	*The Government Inspector*	Piccolo Teatro, Milan
1953			
17 Jan.	Sartre	*The Mechanism*	Piccolo Teatro, Milan
18 Feb.	Pirandello	*The Worst Sacrilege*	Piccolo Teatro, Milan
12 March	Pirandello	*Six Characters in Search of an Author*	Théâtre Marigny, Paris
30 April	Bertolazzi	*Lulu*	Piccolo Teatro, Milan
15 May	Buzzati	*A Clinical Case*	Piccolo Teatro, Milan
7 Oct.	Goldoni	*The Artful Widow*	Teatro La Fenice, Venice
20 Nov.	Shakespeare	*Julius Caesar*	Piccolo Teatro, Milan
18 Dec.	D'Errico	*Six Days*	Piccolo Teatro, Milan
1954			
5 Jan.	Gozzi	*The Crow*	Piccolo Teatro, Milan
19 Jan.	Pirandello	*Triple Bill*	Piccolo Teatro, Milan
24 Feb.	Giraudoux	*The Mad Woman of Chaillot*	Piccolo Teatro, Milan
14 April	Moravia	*The Masquerade*	Piccolo Teatro, Milan
30 April	Praga	*The Ideal Wife*	Piccolo Teatro, Milan
22 June	Bontempelli	*Our Goddess*	Teatro Odeon, Buenos Aires
23 Nov.	Goldoni	The *Villeggiatura* trilogy	Piccolo Teatro, Milan
1955			
13 Jan.	Chekhov	*The Cherry Orchard*	Piccolo Teatro, Milan
21 April	Lorca	*The House of Bernarda Alba*	Piccolo Teatro, Milan
May	Brecht	*The Measures Taken*	Piccolo Teatro, Milan
24 May	Squarzina	*Three Quarters of the Moon*	Piccolo Teatro, Milan
14 Sept.	Prokofiev	*The Fiery Angel*	Teatro la Fenice, Venice
3 Dec.	Bertolazzi	*Our Milan*	Piccolo Teatro, Milan
26 Dec.	Cimarosa	*Il matrimonio segreto*	Piccola Scala, Milan
1956			
10 Feb.	Brecht	*The Threepenny Opera*	Piccolo Teatro, Milan
2 April	Verga	*From Yours to Mine*	Piccolo Teatro, Milan
27 Aug.	Goldoni	*Arlecchino, the Servant of Two Masters*	Royal Lyceum Theatre, Edinburgh
30 Aug.	Pirandello	*Tonight We Improvise*	Royal Lyceum Theatre, Edinburgh
22 Dec.	Prokofiev	*The Fiery Angel*	Teatro alla Scala, Milan
13 April	Zardi	*The Jacobins*	Piccolo Teatro, Milan
16 May	Charpentier	*Louise*	Teatro alla Scala, Milan
2 May	Stravinsky	*The Soldier's Tale*	Piccola Scala, Milan
18 Dec.	Shakespeare	*Coriolanus*	Piccolo Teatro, Milan

Date	Playwright	Title	Theatre
23 Dec.	Ferrari	Goldoni and His Sixteen New Plays	Piccolo Teatro, Milan
1958			
22 Feb.	Brecht	The Good Person of Setzuan	Piccolo Teatro, Milan
19 April	Pirandello	The Mountain Giants	Schauspielhaus, Düsseldorf
2 June	Rota	A Florentine Straw Hat	Piccola Scala, Milan
1959			
27 April	Chekhov	Platonov	Piccolo Teatro, Milan
6 Nov.	Stravinsky	The Soldier's Tale	Teatro della Cometa, Rome
1960			
31 Jan.	Dürrenmatt	The Visit	Piccolo Teatro, Milan
11 Nov.	Bertolazzi	The Egoist	Piccolo Teatro, Milan
1961			
24 Jan.	Brecht	Schweyk in the Second World War	Piccolo Teatro, Milan
1962			
10 May	(double bill) Brecht	The Exception and the Rule	Piccolo Teatro, Milan
	Miller	Memory of Two Mondays	Piccolo Teatro, Milan
1963			
21 April	Brecht	Galileo	Piccolo Teatro, Milan
19 June	Prokofiev	Peter and the Wolf	Teatro alla Scala, Milan
10 July	Goldoni	Arlecchino, the Servant of Two Masters	Villa Litta di Affori, Milan
1964			
29 Feb.	Brecht	Mahagonny	Piccola Scala, Milan
18 May	Salacrou	The Nights of Rage	Piccolo Teatro, Milan
28 Nov.	Goldoni	The Squabbles at Chioggia	Teatro Lirico, Milan
25 Nov.	Kipphardt	In the case of J. Robert Oppenheimer	Piccolo Teatro, Milan
1965			
10 May	Brecht	Bertolt Brecht, Poetry and Songs	Piccolo Teatro, Milan
18 June	Shakespeare	Power Games	Teatro Lirico, Milan
28 June	Mozart	Die Entführung aus dem Serail	Kleines Festspielhaus, Salzburg
1966			
3 May	Cappelli	Two hundred thousand and one	Piccolo Teatro, Milan
12 May	Mascagni	Cavalleria rusticana	Teatro alla Scala, Milan
25 Nov.	Pirandello	The Mountain Giants	Teatro Lirico, Milan
1967			
9 June	Brecht	I, Bertolt Brecht	Piccolo Teatro, Milan
1969			
25 March	Weiss	Song of the Lusitanian Bogey	Teatro Quirino, Rome
23 May	Mozart	Die Entführung aus dem Serail	Teatro della Pergola, Florence
3 June	Beethoven	Fidelio	Teatro Comunale, Florence
1970			
3 July	Brecht	St Joan of the Stockyards	Teatro della Pergola, Florence
12 Nov.	Gorky	The Lower Depths	Teatro Metastasio, Prato

Date	Playwright	Title	Theatre
1971			
4 June	Pallavicini and Vene	*Referendum as to the Pardon or Reprieve of a War Criminal*	Teatro Manzoni, Pistoia
7 Dec.	Verdi	*Simon Boccanegra*	Teatro alla Scala, Milan
1972			
15 May	Mozart	*Die Entführung aus dem Serail*	Teatro alla Scala, Milan
4 Nov.	Shakespeare	*King Lear*	Piccolo Teatro, Milan
1973			
14 Feb.	Brecht	*The Threepenny Opera*	Teatro Metastasio, Prato
30 March	Mozart	*Le nozze di Figaro*	Théâtre du Cour, Versailles
19 May	Brecht	*The Trial of Lucullus*	Teatro Lirico, Milan
13 Aug.	Shakespeare	*Power Games*	Felsenreitschule, Salzburg
1974			
21 May	Chekhov	*The Cherry Orchard*	Piccolo Teatro, Milan
26 July	Mozart	*Die Zauberflöte*	Grosses Festpielhaus, Salzburg
9 Nov.	Goldoni	The *Villeggiatura* trilogy	Burgtheater, Vienna
19 Dec.	Prokofiev	*The Love of Three Oranges*	Teatro alla Scala, Milan
1975			
6 March	Brecht	*I, Bertolt Brecht, No. 2*	Teatro Frascini, Pavia
30 May	Goldoni	*The Little Square*	Piccolo Teatro, Milan
12 Nov.	Shakespeare	*Power Games*	Burgtheater, Vienna
7 Dec.	Verdi	*Macbeth*	Teatro alla Scala, Milan
1976			
19 May	Genet	*The Balcony*	Piccolo Teatro, Milan
22 Dec.	Strehler (Sastre/Brecht)	*The Story of the Abandoned Doll*	Piccolo Scala, Milan
1977			
25 Sept.	Brecht	*The Good Person of Setzuan*	Schauspielhaus, Hamburg
4 Oct.	Goldoni	*Arlecchino, the Servant of Two Masters*	Théâtre Odéon, Paris
1978			
28 June	Shakespeare	*The Tempest*	Teatro Lirico, Milan
16 Dec.	Goldoni	The *Villeggiatura* trilogy	Théâtre Odéon, Paris
1979			
26 Sept	Brecht	*I, Bertolt Brecht, No. 3*	Piccolo Teatro, Milan
18 Dec.	Bertolazzi	*Our Milan*	Teatro Lirico, Milan
1980			
18 June	Strindberg	*Storm*	Piccolo Teatro, Milan
7 Dec.	Verdi	*Falstaff*	Teatro alla Scala, Milan
1981			
4 April	Brecht	*The Good Person of Setzuan*	Teatro Comunale, Modena
7 Dec.	Wagner	*Lohengrin*	Teatro alla Scala, Milan
1982			
5 May	Beckett	*Happy Days*	Piccolo Teatro, Milan
1983			
31 May	Lessing	*Minna von Barnhelm*	Piccolo Teatro, Milan

Date	Playwright	Title	Theatre
1984			
21 Jan.	Mozart	*Die Entführung aus dem Serail*	Théâtre de l'Opéra, Paris
11 Nov.	Corneille	*The (Theatrical) Illusion*	Théâtre Odéon, Paris
1985			
5 May	De Filippo	*Great Magic*	Piccolo Teatro, Milan
1986			
30 June	Strehler (Jouvet)	*Elvire or A Passion for Theatre*	Teatro Studio, Milan
11 Nov.	Brecht	*The Threepenny Opera*	Théâtre du Châtelet, Paris
1987			
14 May	Goldoni	*Arlecchino* (farewell edition)	Piccolo Teatro, Milan
7 Nov.	Mozart	*Don Giovanni*	Teatro alla Scala, Milan
1988			
3 March	Pirandello	*As You Desire Me*	Piccolo Teatro, Milan
30 Dec.	(double bill) Tabucchi	*Time Presses*	Teatro Studio, Milan
	Sarti	*Free*	Teatro Studio, Milan
1989			
18 March	Goethe	Fragments from *Faust, Part I* (first show)	Teatro Studio, Milan
19 March	Goethe	Fragments from *Faust, Part I* (second show)	Teatro Studio, Milan
10 Nov.	Beethoven	*Fidelio*	Théâtre du Châtelet, Paris
1991			
28 April (two shows	Goethe	Fragments from *Faust, Part II*	Teatro Studio, Milan

Notes

1 Towards a theatre of humanity

1 Paolo Grassi, *Quarant'anni di palcoscenico*, ed. Emilio Pozzi (Mursia: Milan, 1977), p. 134.
2 *Ibid.*, p. 149.
3 Ugo Ronfani, *Io, Strehler: Conversazioni: con Ugo Ronfani* (Rusconi: Milan, 1986), p. 65.
4 Giorgio Guazzotti, *Teoria e realtà del Piccolo Teatro di Milano* (Einaudi: Turin, 1965), p. 47.
5 *1947–58 Piccolo Teatro*, ed. Giorgio Strehler (Moneta: Milan, 1958), p. 13.
6 Ronfani, *Io, Strehler*, p. 63.
7 *Ibid.*, pp. 63–4
8 *Ibid.*, p. 64.
9 *Ibid.*, p. 52.
10 *Ibid.*, p. 95.
11 Guazzotti, *Teoria e realtà*, p. 84.
12 Ronfani, *Io, Strehler*, p. 16.
13 Guazzotti, *Teoria e realtà*, p. 82.
14 Ronfani, *Io, Strehler*, p. 191.
15 Giorgio Strehler, *Per un teatro umano* (Feltrinelli; Milan, 1974), p. 50.
16 *Ibid.*, p. 52
17 *Ibid.*, p. 52.
18 *Ibid.*, p. 63
19 Ronfani, *Io, Strehler*, p. 268.
20 *Ibid.*, p. 261
21 *Corriere della Sera*, 3 November 1984.
22 *Libertà*, 24 November 1984.

2 Strehler's style: lyrical realism

1 Anton Chekhov, *Il giardino dei ciliegi*, ed. Luigi Lunari with notes by Giorgio Strehler (Rizzoli: Milan, 1974), p. 155.
2 Ronfani, *Io, Strehler*, pp. 167–8.
3 *Ibid.*, p. 167.
4 *Paese Sera*, 8 May 1974.
5 *La Stampa*, 23 May 1974.
6 *Corriere Lombardo*, 3 December 1955.
7 *Corriere della Sera*, 14 May 1974.
8 Chekhov, *Il giardino*, ed. Lunari, p. 135
9 *Ibid.*, pp. 135–6.
10 *Ibid.*, p. 186.
11 *Ibid.*, p. 133.
12 Roberto de Monticelli in *Corriere della Sera*, 23 May 1974.
13 *Ibid.*
14 Chekhov, *Il giardino*, ed. Lunari, pp. 147–8.
15 *Corriere della Sera*, 14 May 1974.
16 Chekhov, *Il giardino*, ed. Lunari, pp. 142–3.

131

17 *Ibid.*, p. 176.
18 *Ibid.*, p. 189.
19 *Il Messaggero*, 20 December 1979.
20 Programme for *El nost Milan*, p. 23.
21 *Ibid.*, p. 26.
22 *Ibid.*, p. 13.
23 *Ibid.*, p. 27.
24 *Il messaggero*, 20 December 1979.

3 Goldoni, genius at presenting life

1 Carlo Goldoni, *Arlecchino servitore di due padroni*, introduction by Luigi Lunari with a note by Giorgio Strehler; chronology, bibliography and notes by Carlo Pedretti (Rizzoli: Milan, 1979), p. 36.
2 Luigi Lunari, 'Le regie goldoniane di Giorgio Strehler', *Studi goldoniani* 4 (1976), p. 124.
3 Strehler, *Per un teatro umano*. p. 171.
4 *Ibid.*, p. 172.
5 Catherine Douel dell'Agnolla: 'Cinq versions d'"Arlequin"', *Les Voies de la création théâtrale* 16 (Strehler issue, 1989), p. 145.
6 Goldoni, *Arlecchino*, ed. Lunari and others, pp. 37–8
7 *Ibid.*, p. 40.
8 *Ibid.*, pp. 207–8.
9 *Ibid.*, p. 222.
10 Strehler, *Per un teatro umano* pp. 174–5.
11 Goldoni, *Arlecchino*, ed. Lunari and others, pp. 40–1.
12 *Ibid.*, p. 146.
13 *Il giorno*, 14 May 1987.
14 *Ibid.*
15 Gastone Geron in *Il giornale*, 16 May 1987.
16 Fabio Battistini, *Giorgio Strehler* (Gremese: Rome, 1980), p. 92.
17 *Corriere della sera*, 14 October 1950.
18 Gastone Geron, 'L'itinerario goldoniano del "Piccolo"', *Teatro in Europa* (1987), p. 24.
19 Battistini, *Strehler*, p. 111.
20 *Ibid.*, p. 129.
21 Strehler, *Per un teatro umano*, p. 90.
22 Battistini, *Strehler*, p. 66.
23 Carlo Goldoni, *La trilogia della villeggiatura*, introduction by Luigi Lunari and chronology, bibliography and notes by Carlo Pedretti (Rizzoli: Milan, 1982), p. 344.
24 Battistini, *Strehler*, p. 139.
25 Geron, 'L'itinerario goldoniano', p. 26.
26 Carlo Goldoni, *Il campiello*, ed. Luigi Lunari with notes by Giorgio Strehler (Rizzoli: Milan, 1975), p. 36.
27 Goldoni, *La trilogia*, ed. Lunari and Pedretti, p. 32.
28 *Ibid.*, p. 346.
29 Strehler, *Per un teatro umano*, p. 99.
30 *Il campiello*, ed. Lunari, p. 203.
31 *Ibid.*, p. 204.

4 Power games: Strehler and Shakespeare

1 Battistini, *Strehler*, p. 80.
2 *Ibid.*, p. 71.

3 *Ibid.*, p. 116.
4 Programme for *La Tempesta*, 1978, p. 22.
5 Strehler, *Per un teatro umano*, p. 312.
6 *Ibid.*, p. 316.
7 *Ibid.*, p. 122.
8 *Ibid.*, p. 125.
9 *Ibid.*, p. 313.
10 Battistini, *Strehler*, p. 163.
11 *Ibid.*
12 *Ibid.*, p. 198.
13 *Ibid.*, p. 198.
14 Strehler, *Per un teatro umano*, p. 321.
15 Battistini, *Strehler*, p. 253.
16 *Il Giorno*, 29 November 1975.
17 *Ibid.*
18 *Il Giornale*, 21 January 1976.
19 Strehler, *Per un teatro umano*, p. 223.
20 Programme for *Re Lear*, 1972.
21 *Rinascità*, 10 November 1972.
22 William Shakespeare, *Re Lear*, ed. Luigi Lunari with notes by Giorio Strehler and introduction by Agostino Lombardo (Bertani: Verona, 1974), pp. 263–4.
23 *Ibid.*, p. 22.
24 Programme for *La Tempesta*, 1978.

5 Brecht stoppped at Milan

1 Bertolt Brecht, *L'opera da tre soldi*, Giorgio Guazzotti (Capelli: Bologna, 1961), pp. 45–6.
2 *Ibid.*, p. 45.
3 *Film d'Oggi*, 17 May 1956.
4 *La Repubblica*, 12 November 1986.
5 Ronfani, *Io, Strehler*, p. 72.
6 Giorgio Strehler, *Shakespeare, Goldoni, Brecht*, ed. Giovanni Soresi (Il Dialogo: Milan, 1984), p. 115.
7 *Del 'classico' B. B.*, ed. Arturo Lazzari, Il lavoro teatrale (Guanda: Parma, 1970), p. 70.
8 *Film Critica* (February 1962).
9 Ronfani, *Io, Strehler*, p. 192.
10 *Ibid.*, p. 182.
11 *Corriere della Sera*, 12 November 1986.
12 Strehler, *Per un teatro umano*, pp. 118–19.
13 Strehler, *Shakespeare, Goldoni, Brecht*, pp. 114–15.
14 *Tempi Moderni* (April–June 1974).
15 Strehler, *Shakespeare, Goldoni, Brecht*, p. 116.
16 Brecht, *L'opera da tre soldi*, ed. Guazzotti, p. 173.
17 *Corriere d'Informazione*, 1 November 1973.
18 *La Stampa*, 12 November 1986.
19 Ronfani, *Io, Strehler*, p. 70.
20 *Stuttgarter Zeitung*, 1 March 1958.
21 *Ibid.*
22 *Ibid.*
23 *Ibid.*
24 *Corriere della Sera*, 28 September 1977.
25 *Ibid.*

26 *L'Unità*, 11 April 1981.
27 *Corriere della Sera*, 11 April 1981.
28 Bertolt Brecht, *Schweyk nella seconda guerra mondiale*, ed. Luigi Lunari and Raffaele Orlando (Cappelli: Bologna, 1962), p. 14.
29 *Ibid.*, p. 15.
30 *Ibid.*, p. 24.
31 *Ibid.*, pp. 52–3
32 *Ibid.*, p. 57.
33 Guazzotti, *Teoria e realtà*, pp. 154–5.
34 *The Times*, 3 May 1963.
35 Ferruccio Marotti, *Amleto o dell'oxymoron*, (Bulzoni: Rome, 1966), p. 302.
36 *Ibid.*, p. 322.
37 *The Times*, 3 May 1963.
38 Strehler, *Per un teatro umano*, p. 178.
39 *Ibid.*, pp. 306–7.
40 Bertolt Brecht, *Santa Giovanni dei macelli*, ed. Arturo Lazzari and others (Bertani: Verona, 1974), p. 13.
41 *La Stampa*, 6 June 1970.
42 Brecht, *Santa Giovanna*, ed. Lazzari and others, p. 21.

Select bibliography

The following are the major works relating to Strehler. There is nothing in English. I have referred to these books and editions throughout the notes.

Books and articles

Battistini, Fabio. *Giorgio Strehler*. Gremese: Rome, 1980.
Gaipa, Ettore. *Giorgio Strehler*. Cappelli: Bologna, 1959.
Grassi, Paolo. *Quarant'anni di palcoscenico*, ed. Emilio Pozzi. Mursia: Milan, 1977.
Guazzotti, Giorgio. *Teoria e realtà del Piccolo Teatro di Milano*. Einaudi: Turin, 1965.
Lazzari, Arturo, ed. *Del 'classico' B.B.* Il lavoro teatrale, Guanda: Parma, 1970.
Ronfani, Ugo. *Io, Strehler: Conversazioni con Ugo Ronfani*. Rusconi: Milan, 1986.
Strehler, Giorgio. *Per un teatro umano*. Feltrinelli: Milan, 1974.
    Shakespeare, Goldoni, Brecht, ed. Giovanni Soresi. Il Dialogo: Milan, 1984.
    'Schegge di memoria [Fragments of Memory]', *Teatro in Europa* 1 (1987).
    'Operaddio! [Goodbye, Opera!]', *Teatro in Europa* 2 (1987).

Editions

Brecht, Bertolt. *L'opera da tre soldi* [*The Threepenny Opera*]. Photo-chronicle by Ugo Mulas, ed. Giorgio Guazzotti. Cappelli: Bologna, 1961.
    Santa Giovanna dei macelli [*St Joan of the Stockyards*]. Introduction by Arturo Lazzari. Appendix: analysis of the production by Stephan and Claire de Lannoy. Bertani: Verona, 1974.
    Schweyk nella seconda guerra mondiale [*Schweyk in the Second World War*]. Photo-chronicle by Ugo and Mario Mulas, ed. Luigi Lunari and Raffaele Orlando. Cappelli: Bologna, 1962.
Chekhov, Anton. *Il giardino dei ciliegi* [*The Cherry Orchard*]. Ed. Luigi Lunari with notes by Giorgio Strehler. Rizzoli: Milan, 1974.
Goldoni, Carlo. *Arlecchino servitore di due padroni*. Introduction by Luigi Lunari with a note by Giorgio Strehler. Chronology, bibliography and notes by Carlo Pedretti. Rizzoli: Milan, 1979.
    Il campiello. Ed. Luigi Lunari with notes by Giorgio Strehler. Rizzoli: Milan, 1975.
    La trilogia della villeggiatura. Introduction by Luigi Lunari. Chronology, bibliography and notes by Carlo Pedretti. Rizzoli: Milan 1982.
Shakespeare, William. *Re Lear* [*King Lear*]. Ed. Luigi Lunari with notes by Giorgio Strehler. Introduction by Agostino Lombardo. Bertani: Verona, 1974.

Index